# Female Caligula

# Female Caligula

## RANAVALONA
## THE MAD QUEEN OF MADAGASCAR

### KEITH LAIDLER

WILEY

Published in 2005 by       John Wiley & Sons, Ltd, The Atrium, Southern Gate
Chichester, West Sussex, PO19 8SQ, England
Phone      (+44) 1243 779777

Copyright © 2005       Keith Laidler

Email (for orders and customer service enquires): cs-books@wiley.co.uk
Visit our Home Page on www.wiley.co.uk or www.wiley.com

Every Effort has been made to contact all copyright holders. The publishers will be glad to
make good in future editions any errors or omissions brought to their attention.

This publication is designed to provide accurate and authoritative information in regard to
the subject matter covered. It is sold on the understanding that the Publisher is not engaged
in rendering professional services. If professional advice or other expert assistance is
required, the services of a competent professional should be sought.

Keith Laidler has asserted his right under the Copyright, Designs and Patents Act 1988, to
be identified as the author of this work.

### Other Wiley Editorial Offices

John Wiley & Sons, Inc. 111 River Street, Hoboken, NJ 07030, USA

Jossey-Bass, 989 Market Street, San Francisco, CA 94103-1741, USA

Wiley-VCH Verlag GmbH, Pappellaee 3, D-69469 Weinheim, Germany

John Wiley & Sons Australia, Ltd, 33 Park Road, Milton, Queensland, 4064, Australia

John Wiley & Sons (Asia) Pte Ltd, 2 Clementi Loop #02-01, Jin Xing Distripark,
Singapore 129809

John Wiley & Sons Canada Ltd, 22 Worcester Road, Etobicoke, Ontario, Canada, M9W 1L1

Wiley also publishes its books in a variety of electronic formats. Some content that appears
in print may not be available in electronic books.

### Library of Congress Cataloging-in-Publication Data

(to follow)

### British Library Cataloguing in Publication Data

A catalogue record for this book is available from the British Library

ISBN-13   978-0-470-02223-8 (HB) 978-0-470-02226-9 (PB)
ISBN-10   0-470-02223-X (HB) 0-470-02226-4 (PB)

Typeset in $10\frac{1}{2}/13\frac{1}{2}$pt Photina by MCS Publishing Services Ltd, Salisbury, Wiltshire.
Printed and bound in Great Britain by T.J. International, Padstow, Cornwall.
This book is printed on acid-free paper responsibly manufactured from sustainable forestry
in which at least two trees are planted for each one used for paper production.
10 9 8 7 6 5 4 3 2 1

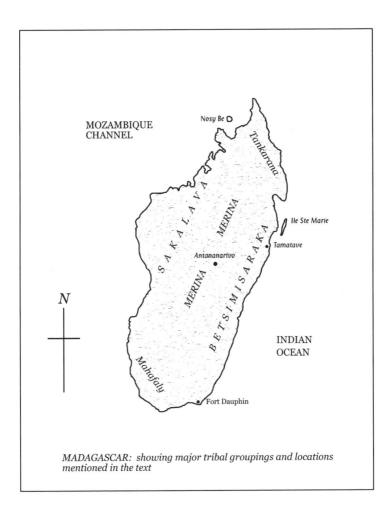

MADAGASCAR: *showing major tribal groupings and locations*
*mentioned in the text*

# Contents

# CHAPTER ONE

# Martyrdom

The seven Christians stood together in the bright sunlight, bound with strong ropes, singing a hymn to their foreign Saviour as the spearmen advanced. Around them a crowd of jostling men, women and children, more than 60,000 strong and dressed in togas of various hues, yelled and jeered at the forlorn expression of faith by the condemned. Hucksters moved through the crowd, calling out their wares, selling snacks and drinks for the entertainment, and noting too a distinct sense of disappointment in their customers. The mob was angry. They felt cheated: they had come to enjoy the destruction of the hated sect, to see its adherents run screaming and panic-stricken from the spears, not to watch them taking their slaughter meekly like so many placid sheep. There was little entertainment to be had in this lack-lustre performance.

It had been the same just moments before, when a score of the Christians had been burned alive, the same calm acceptance of their fate, the same hateful hymn singing. Nevertheless, they cheered enthusiastically as the spears were driven home and, one by one, the men and women fell and writhed on the sandy ground, their hymn fading slowly into silence, replaced by the groans and shrieks of the dying. Above the still-squirming bodies, on a ridge, a score of crosses stood in mute witness, carrying their ghastly burdens, some of whom still lived despite the day and a half they had hung upon the wood. The stench of the charnel house pervaded the natural amphitheatre where the grotesque show was taking place, and the baying, blood-drunk crowd, the massed ranks of soldiery and the crucifixions, silhouetted along the skyline, gave the unmistakable impression of Rome at its worst.

And yet this was no persecution under Nero or Diocletian, intent on entertaining the mob and wiping out the followers of Christ. The motive was identical, but Rome was far away, some 6,000 kilometres to the north and 1,500 years in the past. This was Africa, the year was 1836, and the author of this holocaust was a diminutive, light-skinned woman of middle years, Ranavalona-Manjaka Queen of Madagascar, known to her subjects as The Great Lake Supplying All Water, the Great Glory, The Eye of God on Earth or, more simply, *Ma Dieu*. Under her despotic rule, hundreds of thousands of her people perished: at least a third, and possibly half, of Madagascar's entire population were murdered, starved or simply worked to death by her express command. She made the island a fortress, and led a constant, ruthless struggle against European colonial ambitions. Her hatred of foreigners was legendary, and those few Europeans fortunate enough to have made her acquaintance and lived knew her as a sadistic monster, a gorgon, whose cruelty and debauched life recalled the worst excesses of ancient Rome. She possessed, said one, 'the appetites of a Messalina and the temperament of a Caligula'. And this, if she is remembered at all, is how European history commemorates her reign, as the rule of the 'Female Caligula'.

But, as ever, the story is far more complicated than any simple soubriquet can convey. There is no doubt that the tales of sadism, debauchery and mass murder are true, and that before she died she probably had descended into madness. But Ranavalona-Manjaka was, as much as anyone, a product of her temperament, upbringing and the times in which she lived. And those times were terrible, fraught with internal and external dangers, intrigue, betrayal, and the constant threat of invasion by colonial powers who, while perhaps less barbarous, were every bit as ruthless as the natives they tried to subdue. Just as destructive to morality and sanity was the threat that has always sprung from wielding absolute power, and the even greater hazards that attend being worshipped as God on Earth.

# CHAPTER TWO

# The Great Red Island

**D**espite lying only 450 kilometres off the African mainland, the island of Madagascar remained devoid of humans until some time just after the birth of Christ. There is enormous irony in the fact that humanity evolved from ape men such as *Australopithecus africanus* just a thousand miles away on the African savannah, and yet it was not until humans had spread out over the entire globe, colonising such inhospitable regions as the Arctic and the far reaches of America, that they finally discovered and settled on the Great Red Island. The civilisations of Sumeria and Mycaenae, the dynasties of Egypt and Assyria, the Olmec of Central America, the Shang of China, the Harapan civilisation of India – all blossomed and decayed before a human set foot on Madagascar.

Equally astonishing is that when Madagascar was finally settled, it was not by Africans but by seafarers from far beyond the Indian Ocean, Malay and Polynesian sailors who had made the 6,400-kilometre crossing from the Indonesian archipelago. Anthropological and ethnographic data appear to confirm that these first immigrants did not descend upon Madagascar in piecemeal fashion; they most probably arrived as a single fleet, or at least over a relatively short space of time. Whether the colonists braved a direct Indian Ocean crossing or eschewed the dangers of the Deep and took the longer, but safer, route through coastal waters remains unknown. The evidence of Indonesian-style craft scattered all along the northern rim of the Indian Ocean argues for the latter course. These Malay–Polynesian settlers probably took several years to make their journey, travelling and trading slowly westwards along the coasts of India and Arabia before turning their prows south and moving gradually down the East African coast towards their final goal. But the journey was worth their pains. What they found when they arrived was an island paradise, lying athwart the Tropic of Capricorn and with a splendid variety of climates and topography to suit all temperaments.

Madagascar is the fourth largest island in the world, 587,040 square kilometres in extent, with the dark forests of the coast climbing in two steps or plateaus from the low-lying eastern plains onto the steep bluffs and deep valleys of the central highlands. To the north rises the Tsaratanana Massif, its pointed peaks the remains of long-dead volcanos, while on the west lies a narrow strip of lowland with many protected harbours and well-watered, fertile plains. Almost all the country at that time was covered in dense forest, lush and verdant, except for the southern-most region of the island, where much-reduced annual rainfall had resulted in a desert and semi-desert ecosystem.

The land itself was filled to bursting with unique flora and fauna, strange bromeliads, cycads, orchids and other botanical wonders unlike anything found in either Africa or Asia. Madagascar had not always been an island; for millennia it had been joined to the western flank of the African mainland. But around 50 million years ago massive geologic forces separated the island from the continent, since when it had slowly drifted to the east, creating the Mozambique Channel. This natural barrier, over 450 miles wide, has effectively isolated the primitive wildlife of Madagascar from invasion by more advanced forms that evolved later in Africa. The unique 'time capsule' that resulted has produced a natural laboratory where Madagascan life-forms have evolved over scores of millions of years at their own pace and in ways utterly at variance with the dominant flow of evolution on our planet.

Perhaps the most surprising group of creatures on the island are the prosimians, better known as lemurs. Primates like us, the lemurs are a relict from the days before the evolution of monkeys, apes or humankind. For a brief space of time (geologically speaking) the lemurs were the most advanced primates on the planet. They thrived in the forests that covered much of the Earth at this time and migrated to many parts of the world, evolving into numerous ecological niches. But with the coming of the more advanced primate species they lost out in the competition for *lebensraum* all across the face of the globe, and gradually disappeared. Except in Madagascar, where the moat-like Mozambique Channel acted as a barrier to prevent invasion by the more evolved monkeys and apes. The island became the last bastion of lemurkind. Here alone the lemurs were free from competition and at liberty to radiate out into all the many ecosystems the island had to offer. They were not slow to take advantage of the opportunity. Lemurs now include the smallest primate genus, *Microcebus* (the mouse lemurs), while until very recently (and perhaps made extinct by the advent of humans) there were lemurs as large as chimpanzees.

Captain William Keeling of the East India Company's ship *Dragon* was the first European to catch sight of some of these unique Madagascan inhabitants and record his observations. In 1608, as he explored the mouth of the Onilahy River in south-west Madagascar, he noted:

*In the woods neere about the river, is a great store of beasts, as big*
*as Munkies, ash-coloured, with a small head, long tail like a Fox,*
*garled with white and black, the furre very fine.*

Captain Keeling had seen the ring-tailed lemur, a social species
and one of the commonest forms on the island. Over 150 years
later Pierre Sonnerat, the French *Naturaliste Pensionnaire du Roi*,
described the largest of the living lemurs in his multivolume
account of his travels, naming the beast by the Malagasy word
*indri*, a title by which it is still known to this day. It is an
unfortunate soubriquet; Monsieur Sonnerat was apparently quite
unaware that the name he thought he heard applied to the beast
was simply a Malagasy exclamation, meaning 'There it is!'.

If the lemurs had benefited from the isolation of Madagascar's
forests, the same could not be said for its first human inhabitants.
They were not left to enjoy the benefits of the island for long.
After the initial discovery and colonisation, word of its wonders
percolated across the oceans to both Africa and the Far East, and
more and more cultures and races of humankind took ship to the
Great Red Island, intent on making this tropical Eden their home.
The human ethnic mix of Madagascar was set to become as
singular as its wildlife and to drive the creation of a society seen
nowhere else on Earth.

# CHAPTER THREE

# Polynesians and Pirates

The early Malay–Polynesian seafarers who first settled the island were joined by further waves of East Asian immigrants, especially during the ninth century AD, when the Empire of Srivajaya, based on the island of Sumatra, ruled the waves throughout most of the Indian Ocean. The colonists brought with them the foodstuffs of their former homelands, rice, peppers and mangos, and even today farming in Madagascar resembles more the paddy fields and irrigation ditches of East Asia than the agriculture of sub-Saharan African. Some of the more productive Asian farming methods gradually diffused to the mainland and, apparently newly aware of this novel landmass to the east, ethnic Africans (mainly Bantu-speaking tribespeople) now began to join the already established Asians on this highly fertile island in the Eastern Sea. Swahili-speaking traders also crossed the Mozambique Channel to settle. They were followed, at about the same time, by Arab traders from Oman, who began to visit the island in considerable numbers, bringing with them the horrors of the slave trade and a version of the Arab alphabet that survived until very recently in the scrolls of a southern Malagasy tribe, the Mahafaly. Shortly thereafter (around the eleventh century) the first arrivals of the Antalaotra ('sailors') came ashore. These were Islamised Swahili-speaking settlers from the Comoros Islands, some 300 kilometres to the north-west of Madagascar. The Antalaotra established themselves on the north-west of the island, and for the next few centuries were able to control maritime trade with both mainland Africa and points east.

These successive waves of immigration resulted in a mosaic of tribal and ethnic groupings that, in time-honoured human fashion, fought among each other for supremacy. Malagasy history for the next few centuries consists primarily of the formation and dissolution of alliances, and of almost continuous conflict in one part or another of the country, with each tribal group pursuing the dream of hegemony, striving endlessly to subdue the remaining clans and gain ultimate control of the Great Red Island.

The final ingredient in Madagascar's racial potpourri arrived relatively late in the day in the form of European colonists and outlaws. Madagascar had been known to the Portuguese since 1500, when Captain Diego Dias's galleon, bound for the Indies, had been blown from its intended course and he had sighted Madagascar's southern coast. (Dias had named the island 'Sao Lourenco', but the new name failed to stick.) This was the beginning of the age of European imperialism, and Africa remained the Dark Continent, almost completed isolated from European influence – vast, unknown and malign. Some few ports around the coast of the enormous landmass were known, but for the most part Africa's very bulk deterred the Europeans from further exploration. As an island, albeit of considerable extent, Madagascar appeared much more amenable to control. The Portuguese were not slow to realise its importance as a base and staging post in the dangerous but highly profitable trade in eastern spices such as nutmeg, cloves and mace. Over the next hundred years, various attempts were made by these intrepid sailors to plant colonies on the island, and to wrest control of the sea trade from the Antalaotra. However, the natives proved extremely tenacious of their mercantile and territorial rights, and all such enterprises came to nothing.

The English, too, tried colonies along the south-west coast, notably in the Bay of Antongil. But they were no more successful than the Portuguese in establishing themselves along Madagascar's green shoreline, due primarily to high mortality from tropical disease and the steadfast hostility of the native population to any colonial incursion.

Early in 1642 the French tried their hand. By order of Cardinal Richelieu himself, a clerk of the French East India Company, Monsieur Jacques de Pronis, was sent to the Great Red Island, carrying with him letters patent granting him 'the exclusive privilege to adjudicate in the island of Madagascar and other islands adjacent and to set up colonies there'. A year later de Pronis founded the colony and bastion of Fort Dauphin, which both Richelieu and the French merchant adventurers saw as a vital staging post for French expansion eastwards into the spice-rich Indies.

Despite all these numerous attempts at colony building, the opportunity actually to engage with the Malagasy native inhabitants was all but ignored, and very little was known about the island or the traditions and beliefs of its population. The ignorance of the would-be colonists was finally remedied in 1658 when de Pronis's successor, Etienne de Flacourt, published a *History of the Large Island of Madagascar*, a volume that gave the first extensive account of the island and its people, and even included a dictionary of Malagasy words and idioms. This seminal work was to remain a rich mine of information concerning Madagascar and its people for more than two centuries.

Unlike earlier attempts (and with the help, perhaps, of Flacourt's new knowledge) the colony at Fort Dauphin was a success. It survived for more than thirty years, due in large measure to the great pains the colonists took to maintain friendly relations with the local tribes, especially the Antanosy, whose territory surrounded Fort Dauphin. Nevertheless, as time went on, a degree of Gallic arrogance coupled with the Malagasy's historical distrust of foreigners resulted in a gradual deterioration of relations. The Antanosy came to resent the French presence, and in 1674 they suddenly rose up against the colonists. More than half the population of Fort Dauphin were massacred, and the survivors fled the Great Red Island for the safer shores of Reunion. They never returned. Like the rest of the European powers, the French had had enough. It would be more than fifty years before the tricolour was once again hoisted on Malagasy soil.

Where government-inspired initiatives failed, European private enterprise proved spectacularly successful. In the early 1700s, just over 100 years before Ranavalona's birth, a succession of pirate 'brotherhoods' set down roots on Madagascar, making the island their home base for forays into the Indian Ocean. Sometime before this, in 1614, French buccaneers had briefly used the island as a base for raids into the Red Sea. But the privateers' numbers did not really increase until around 80 years later, when plying their bloody trade on the 'Spanish Main' became both less profitable and more dangerous. This was due to a fall-off in the number of treasure galleons ploughing their way between the Caribbean and the Iberian Peninsula, and to the zealous efforts of British, American and French men-o'-war, sent to the West Indies solely to search out and destroy the sea raiders.

Many pirate crews sailed for calmer waters and richer pickings in the Indian Ocean. Their main hunting ground lay to the north, in the crowded shipping lanes of the Red Sea and Persian Gulf, but Madagascar was an ideal base of operations. The island was attractive for its abundant sheltered bays and almost limitless supplies of fresh food and water. Best of all, no European power held sway on the island, and a band of bold, resolute *boucaniers* could carve out a safe haven for themselves without much trouble. Ile Ste Marie, set just off the north-east coast, was their favourite haunt, and by 1700 upwards of seventeen pirate vessels and 1,500 men had made it their home port. Other pirate bands, each under the command of a single leader, known as a 'king', established enclaves at Ranter Bay, St Augustine's Bay, Johnna Island, Fort Dauphin and Charnock's Point. But perhaps the most famous of these pirate havens was the legendary (and perhaps mythical) pirate 'republic' of Libertalia.

The account of this buccaneers' Utopia is to be found only in one book: *A General History of Pyrates* by Captain Charles Johnson. Libertalia was said to have been founded by Captain Misson, a French pirate whom Johnson portrays as part warrior, part philosopher, and a man who ran his ship on strictly republican principles. It must be said that, apart from Johnson's account, there is no record of a Captain Misson anywhere near Madagascan waters; but the existence of the putative Admiral of the pirate republic, Thomas Tew, is well attested in contemporary records. King William III's Royal Warrant of 1695, which authorised Captain Kidd to hunt down buccaneers, specifically notes Thomas Tew as a 'wicked and ill-disposed person', a rogue well fitted to appear as the main attraction at Execution Dock. However, the Crown may well have been indulging in a little character assassination, as other reports suggest that Tew was well known for his kindness. Some even report that many of the ships he stopped, on hearing him named as commander of the opposing vessel, were so confident of being well treated that they gave themselves up without a fight.

Ironically, Captain Kidd the pirate hunter himself turned sea wolf soon after setting out to destroy Tew and the other outlaws, and he too based himself for a while on Madagascar, before taking his crew back to the Americas and famously burying an immense treasure on Gardiner's or Deer island. He was finally captured in 1700 and 'danced the Tyburn jig' on the scaffold a year later. His body was not buried, but was well tarred to preclude decomposition and gibbeted by the Thames, where it hung swaying in the wind for many years as a warning to all would-be corsairs.

Like Kidd, Captain Tew had also originally sailed as a legal 'privateer', on a mission to attack a French 'factory' at Goori, in the Gambia. But halfway across the Atlantic he and his crew decided that the freebooter's life would suit them better and they turned their ship towards the Cape of Good Hope and the pirate haven of Madagascar. While on the island, Tew met, and clashed with, Libertalia's Captain Misson, and the pair agreed to a duel to decide their differences. Only the intercession of a defrocked Italian priest brought about a reconciliation, which eventually led to Tew's commission as Admiral of Libertalia's fleet. (The defrocked priest, in recognition of his tact and diplomacy, is said to have been appointed Secretary of State of the budding republic.)

Pirating paid off for Thomas Tew. After several successful seasons he sailed for home waters and established himself at Rhode Island with a considerable fortune, the size of which might be judged from the fact that he sent the owners of the boat he had 'requisitioned' at the start of his buccaneering career a thank-you gift of *fourteen times* the ship's worth. Had he stayed in the Americas, Tew might have enjoyed what few buccaneers achieved – a safe and prosperous old age. But the call of his old life proved too great: the former Admiral of Libertalia accepted an offer to command a vessel that was being sent to ravage in the Indian Ocean. There, he attempted to seize a massive ship of the Great Moghul Emperor. During the ensuing onslaught, 'a shot carried away the rim of Tew's belly, who held his bowels with his hands for some space' before finally collapsing dead on the deck.

Whatever the truth of Captain Kidd's treasure or Tew's adventures in the Utopian republic of Libertalia, there is no doubting a considerable buccaneering presence on the Great Red Island. Freebooters from as far afield as North America, the Caribbean and most of western Europe were, for many years, prominent members of Madagascar society, especially along the many-harboured eastern seaboard. Some, like the ill-starred Captain Tew, eventually took their ships and plunder back to home waters, with one former pirate being credited with the introduction of Malagasy rice into South Carolina during the eighteenth century. But many of the sea robbers remained on the island, where they made their presence felt in both political and genetic terms. The children of pirate fathers and Malagasy mothers became so numerous that they soon formed the dominant strain in the north-east of the island, where they eventually developed into a separate caste or tribe known as the Zana Malata ('mullattos').

In 1712 this mixing of genes threw up a young man known as Ratsimilaho, the son of an English pirate, 'Tom', and a Madagascan princess, Antavaratra Rahena. Although of tender years (he was only eighteen), Ratsimilaho succeeded in forming the Zana Malata into an unstoppable military force. The exact identity of Ratsimilaho's father remains a subject for dispute, with some researchers fathering the young man by the English buccaneer Thomas White. Unfortunately, Thomas White could not have had a child in Madagascar much before 1705, which does not fit with Ratsimilaho's age of eighteen in 1712. It is much more likely that, as Malagasy tradition asserts, it was none other than our old friend, Libertalia's renowned Admiral Thomas Tew, who had sired the boy during his time on the island.

Ratsimilaho had not only inherited a bold and fearless temperament from his father, he had also fallen heir to a substantial amount of money, deriving ultimately from the booty his father had amassed. He used this to purchase substantial numbers of western muskets and gunpowder, which he distributed among his followers, developing a nucleus of trained warriors. At that time the Zana Malata were oppressed by Ramanano, a warlord who led a confederation of tribes known as the Tsikoa ('the invincible ones'). Over a period of months, using his musket-wielding shock troops and by judiciously allying himself with other subjected peoples such as the southern Antatsimo, Ratsimilaho finally subdued the Tsikoa, forcing their chief Ramanano to pay annual reparations of five slaves and fifty cows for a period of five years. A hero to all who had suffered under the yoke of the Tsikoa, this son of a pirate was elected king over all the central and northern peoples of Madagascar's east coast, who took the name Betsimisaraka, meaning 'those who stand united'.

While Ratsimilaho and his Betsimisaraka warriors ruled over the east of the island, another power had long held sway in the west. Since the beginning of the seventeenth century the Menabe kingdom had gradually been expanding northwards from its western base, suppressing and incorporating smaller tribes into its realm until it eventually reached to the mouth of the Tsiribihina River. Under King Andriamisara I the Menabe continued their expansion and set up a new capital, Bengy, on the banks of the Sakalava river, from which the new 'empire' eventually took its name.

The Sakalava ('People of the Long Valley') are thought to be more African in descent than most of the other Malagasy ethnic groups, and linguistic and ethnographic evidence points to their being originally immigrants from the Mwene Mutapa, a mainland kingdom that rose to power by controlling a number of important trade routes in south-east Africa. It is true that the remains of Sakalava royalty of the Maroserana clan were treated in a typically mainland African fashion: they were held in elaborate reliquaries and their memories invested with divine status. A vertebra of the dead king's neck, a nail from his right hand and a lock of his hair were placed inside a hollow crocodile tooth and 'carefully kept along with the similar relics of his predecessors in a house set apart for the purpose'. In addition, royally appointed spirit mediums were used as vessels into which the shades of dead ancestors could descend to make known their wishes. This explicit connection with his deceased forebears greatly strengthened the king's rule and helped to forge the Sakalava into an unstoppable force that conquered most of the western and northern regions of Madagascar. Although the late 1700s were to see much of its power wane due to rebellion and factional strife, throughout most of the eighteenth century the Sakalava empire continued to retain at least a nominal hold on much of Madagascar's western and northern coasts.

The power base for both of these tribal confederations, the Sakalava and the Betsimisaraka 'empires', and also for the smaller ethnic groupings of the south, lay in the fertile, low-lying regions of the coast. Here the living was easy, the ground fertile, the coastal waters alive with fish, and trade with both European and Arab traders an added economic advantage. The centre of the island remained, for the most part, as much *terra incognita* to the coastlanders as to the foreign nations who increasingly visited the Great Red Island. Despite frequent incursions, no one had fully conquered the tribes in the mountainous interior of the island. The terrain was difficult and dangerous and, as far as the coastal tribes were concerned, except as a source of slaves there was very little of value in the lands of the high plateau. But it was here, at the end of the eighteenth century, that a distant relative of Ranavalona, an insignificant sub-king of a seemingly unimportant mountain tribe, the Hova, was slowly increasing in strength, and dreaming his own dreams of conquest.

# CHAPTER FOUR

# Beneath The Heavens

The Hova were Malay in origin, which they betrayed in their light complexions and long, dark wavy hair. They were late arrivals to Madagascar, probably arriving some time in the middle of the fourteenth or fifteenth century. All of the lowland areas had been settled by this time and they were forced to make their way into the mountainous interior to find living space. Even here they discovered that the land was already settled, by the Vazimba, the legendary 'white dwarves' of the interior, who were said to live by fishing in the region's many rivers and marshlands. During the time of King Ralambo (c. 1575–1610), the Hova gradually displaced the Vazimba from their territory and in an early example of ethnic cleansing they apparently slaughtered all they found, for within a few hundred years the 'white dwarves' lived only in the oral traditions of the Malagasy tribes. And while the swamps of the uplands were regarded as 'wilderness' by the coastlanders, for the Malayan Hova, with their tradition of rice growing in marshy 'paddy fields', the highland region was all they could have asked for. In a very short time the swamps had been transformed into productive paddies, and the new Hova lands were filled with people.

King Ralambo was the first to unite his tribe under a single ruler. In token of their new-found unity, he renamed the tribe the Merina, giving the land they had conquered the title Imerina. He introduced a number of social and political institutions among his people to reinforce his centralised rule. Among other innovations Ralambo advanced was a caste system that divided the Merina into three sections: nobles, commoners and slaves. Ralambo's 'royal' ancestors were granted divine status, and were said to be intimately concerned with the fate of the nation. In the *Famadihana* ritual, the turning of the dead, their bodies were exhumed months after burial, cleaned, rewrapped in clean silken shrouds, and reburied amid festivities in their honour.

Ceremonial circumcision of all males of the royal line served to further distance and elevate the new monarchy from its subjects. Just as important was the establishment of a council of twelve *sampy*, guardians of the state amulets that functioned, as with the Crown Jewels of the British monarchy, as effective symbols of the new state. King Ralambo obtained muskets from the coast, which greatly enhanced the nation's defences against the increasing attacks they were experiencing from lowland tribes, many of whom, worried by the highlander's increasing strength, had begun mounting slaving expeditions against the Hova/ Merina. He also rescinded an ancient taboo on cows, so that his army of beef-eating warriors developed an enviable reputation as formidable fighters. It was Ralambo's son, Adrianjaka, who seized the Blue Forest (Analamanga), one of the last bastions of the Vazimba, and made it the capital of the new kingdom, naming the city Antananarivo ('city of the thousand warriors'). Following this, the Merina royalty waxed strong and for many years held themselves the equals, or betters, of any of the noble houses of the coast.

Perhaps in retaliation for their enemy's perceived hubris, the coastal tribes tell a different tale of the Hova immigration, and of the origins of the Merina royal family. According to this tradition, on arrival in Madagascar at Antongil Bay, the Hova people were immediately conquered by two local tribes and sent as slaves to the central highlands. Later, the Sakalava tribe assumed control and put them to work, again as slaves, draining marshes and building irrigation ditches for their masters' paddy fields. In a further insulting twist to Hova pride, the Merina royalty are held to be simply an outlawed branch of the Sakalava nobility. The story goes that a minor Sakalava chieftain, from the island of Nosy Be, discovered to his horror that his mistress had been seduced by one of his own sons. The crime was great and called for the death sentence. But the boy was the king's favourite, and instead of the miscreant being executed he was exiled to the central highlands, which the coastal tribes claim was used as a Malagasy version of Siberia – an inhospitable and altogether awful place, fit only for felons and murderers. Out of love for the young man, his grandparents are said to have followed him to his place of exile, where his grandmother, Queen Rangita, and her daughter, Queen Rafohy, established a court and began the Merina dynasty that was to hold power among the Hova for many centuries.

Whatever the truth of Hova origins, by the late 1700s the unity imposed by King Ralambo had crumbled, and the Merina had become divided into a number of sub-kingdoms in the central Malagasy highlands, continually at war either between themselves or with the more powerful coastal tribes. In 1787 one of these petty monarchs, the ruler of the tiny kingdom of Ambohimanga, died (or 'retired', as the Hova more delicately put it). According to ancient custom, the small realm was to be further sub-divided between five legal heirs, a young man named Andrianampoinimerina and four of his male cousins. But Andrianampoinimerina was an extremely ambitious individual, and it soon became obvious that he set very little store by Hova tradition. Moving swiftly, he removed his four cousins from power and then from life, leaving himself the sole and undisputed heir. When he ascended to the throne of Ambohimanga, he rejoiced in a title that comprised 23 glorious syllables: Andrianampoinimerinandriantsimitoviaminandriampanjaka (meaning 'the beloved prince of Imerina who surpasses the reigning prince').

Vigorous and cunning, the only description we have of this formidable man is by a European slave trader, Barthelemy Hugon, who saw him in 1808, when he was probably over sixty. He described the king as 'very ugly, with straight hair, having the appearance of a Malay'. Ugly or not, through a series of lightning campaigns the new monarch gave evidence of his courage by fighting in the front ranks with his men, leading them to victory after victory until Andrianampoinimerina had taken possession of most of the central highlands.

However, despite his success in war, it was less by his conquests than by his powers of organisation that Andrianampoinimerina distinguished himself to history. He centralised all power in himself, fortified his borders with settlers and, quickly realising the superiority of foreign weaponry, took great pains to acquire European firearms. Under his rule, the Merina ceased to pay tribute to the Sakalava tribe that had traditionally dominated the highland clans. And ominously for the other Malagasy kingdoms, once Andrianampoinimerina had consolidated his power in this region, he restlessly cast about for more realms to conquer. As a result of these successes, and his continuing ambition, the Sakalava and several other tribes actively conspired to bring about his death and there were several attempts on his life.

Nevertheless, it was not from the enemy but his own kinsfolk that the greatest threat came. Like all dynastic clans, there was fierce jealousy and competition between the members of royal stock, and intrigue and murder were as much a staple of life at the Merina court as they were for the Caesars of the Roman Imperium or China's numerous emperors. It was an attempt on the life of Andrianampoinimerina by one of his uncles that was to alter the balance of power within the Merina hierarchy – and bring a young girl from obscurity to a position from which she might dare to dream of seizing supreme power for herself.

Andrianjafy was the king's maternal uncle, and he too had designs on the throne. Early in Andrianampoinimerina's career, he conceived a plan to murder his ambitious nephew by the simple expedient of pushing him over a steep precipice at Ambohimanga, close to a path where the king loved to walk. One man discovered the intrigue by chance and quickly reported the plotters to his master, forcing the conspirators to abandon their plans. When he came to the throne of the Merina and was secure in his power, Andrianampoinimerina rewarded this loyal follower by adopting his daughter Ranavalona as his own and betrothing her, at the age of twenty-two, to his favourite son, the sixteen-year-old Radama.

But there was more to this act than simply bestowing a royal title on the daughter of a loyal subject. Like many African tribes, the Merina traced their descent through the distaff side. Tradition precluded any concerns about the legitimacy or otherwise of a child born to a royal princess, for there can be no query about the mother of a child, whereas paternity is always in doubt and, as the old phrase has it, 'it is a wise man who knows his father'. In keeping with many royal families, especially the Egyptian pharaohs, the Merina also practised brother–sister marriage, a (to us) incestuous union that further ensured the purity of the *sang real* down the generations. So, by marrying Ranavalona to her adopted brother, Andrianampoinimerina was bringing her family line within the sacred circle of the Merina monarchy, for he had already arranged that his son Radama was to succeed him to the kingship; and further, that whatever children resulted from this marriage between his son and his adopted daughter were to take precedence over all others in any claim to the throne.

Such dynastic provision was vital for, like his predecessors, when Radama finally succeeded to the purple in 1810 he already maintained a harem of biblical proportions; and as he was reputedly very free with his affections, he was the father of several children. As with the monarchs of the Bible, each descendant felt that, could they but win through to the throne, they would be able to claim some legitimacy to rule. Intrigue and conspiracy were the inevitable result, and Ranavalona was to spend much of her teens immersed in this febrile and plot-filled atmosphere, an environment that can only have soured and corrupted whatever natural benevolence and integrity she may have possessed as a child. In such a milieu only the ruthless and the cunning survive, and the lessons of the court will not have been lost on the intelligent young girl that fate had forced, willy-nilly, to the very centre of Merina governance.

# CHAPTER FIVE

# The Malagasy Napoleon

In her youth Ranavalona was, by all accounts, a beautiful young woman, extremely supple and well proportioned, a 'smooth polished body ... with the feet and hands of a child, and the small round head of a haughty she-cat'. Belying her Malay ancestry, her complexion was warm, somewhere between orange and copper, with just a hint of violet. Her face was framed by long, dark, lustrous tresses that she normally kept plaited, her nose was 'short but not flat', her dark eyes lightly slanted, 'sparkling with cunning', and her lips full and sensuous, which sorted well with the voluptuous temperament she was to reveal later in life. Nor, even in her teens, was she ignorant of the delights of Venus: in the culture in which she grew up it was not at all unusual for a girl of eleven to have lost her virginity. There was no shame in this, rather the contrary: the girl was appreciated for the experience she had acquired in the carnal delights and was much sought after.

Despite her undoubted beauty, and prominence as 'mother of the heir' (should she eventually conceive), there is no evidence that Ranavalona figured largely in King Radama's affections. She was recognised as holding the high rank of *Roambinifolovavy*, one of the twelve senior wives of the sovereign, but she was certainly not his favourite wife. Nor was she destined to bear him any children. It may be that their relationship was soured almost from the beginning when the political realities of the Merina court forced Radama, on his accession, to order the execution of several of Ranavalona's close relatives. The young girl might in theory, and by adoption, be the 'daughter' of Andrianampoinimerina, but she knew to which bloodline she truly belonged, and she can only have revolted against the sudden deaths of her blood kin. It was a resentment on which she appears to have brooded, and for which the relatives of her adopted father would pay dearly in time to come.

For the moment she could only watch as her husband consolidated his hold on power and strove to accomplish his father's dying admonition: 'Let the sea be the borders of your rice field, O Radama.' Radama I was, according the French traveller Leguevel de Lacombe,

> short and slender but well proportioned and of pleasing appearance; his features were those of a Malay, but more delicate; his skin was whiter and smoother, his eyes lively and sparkling. His nervous tics and quick jerky speech revealed straightaway the petulance of his character.

Indeed, if the new monarch had one weakness it was that his upbringing as the favourite son of an autocratic monarch had left him spoilt and impatient. Restraint was to him an unknown word, and his lack of discipline in his pursuit of the *dolce vita* undoubtedly contributed to what was to be an early end to his reign. And yet strangely, Radama proved himself to be a master diplomat and warrior, fully deserving his later title of the Malagasy Napoleon.

His accession, at the early age of seventeen, led to revolts throughout his kingdom, which he put down with great rigour. His first campaigns of conquest were also almost invariably successful. He even succeeded in subduing the pugnacious Vohibato tribe, in a campaign that ended at the siege of their 'impregnable' village of Ifandana. Realising that a frontal assault would be suicidal, Radama decided to starve the defenders out, but despite the lack of food, the Vohibato refused to surrender. Instead, en masse, they left the safety of their high-walled bastion and, in plain sight, began covering one another's eyes with scarves and bandanas. Then, as Radama's men watched in amazement, the entire unseeing throng of men, women and children danced together on the edge of the bluff that protected their homes until, in ones and twos, they slipped from the crag and were broken and mangled on the jagged rocks below. Even to this day, a disintegrating mound of human bones proclaims the spot where over 3,000 perished in this macabre dance of death.

Even as he extended his borders, King Radama was aware of the Europeans' appetite for new colonies, their insatiable expansionist policies and the need to counter their advances. In foreign relations Radama proved to be the equal of the colonial powers. He early realised the danger posed by both the British and French interests in Madagascar, and by adeptly playing off the competing interests of the two colonial powers, he was able to extend Merina power over virtually all the island. This he did primarily by persuading the British to supply him with arms and military training.

At that time, the British were deeply committed to their Indian Empire and the recently acquired (1798) colony of Ceylon. In 1810 they attacked and captured the remaining French possessions in the Indian Ocean, the islands of Bourbon (renamed Reunion) and Ile de France, which reverted to its original name of Mauritius. The British, led by the newly appointed Governor of Mauritius, Robert Townsend Farquhar, were well aware of Madagascar's strategic position in the region. They knew also that they did not possess the resources to annex the Great Red Island themselves, but equally, they were adamant that France should not find any opportunity to do so. Farquhar commissioned a survey of all available knowledge on the island, and in one unsigned memorandum the eventual policy of the British Government is prefigured:

> Can it be hoped that the chiefs and the inhabitants will submit of their own free will to the English? This cannot be hoped for. If a single monarch were in authority over the whole extent of the island, he might possibly be won over to yield his crown to the King and people of Great Britain.

So to keep the French, and other European nations, at arm's length, Farquhar needed a strong native king to support. After scrupulous research he found the very man he needed in Radama, acknowledged by all to be the most puissant of the Malagasy princes. Farquhar made his first approach discreetly, sending a French former slave trader, Jacques Chardenoux, to Radama's capital to sound out the king's response to his proposals, which included the offer of an alliance with His Britannic Majesty, the suggestion that members of Radama's council should visit Mauritius, that members of the royal family could be educated on the British possession and, most sensitive of all, that the king might consider a curtailment of the slave trade in his domains.

Though he was naturally cautious on this first visit by the British representatives, King Radama could see the benefits of an alliance with the powerful country that had so comprehensively defeated his hero, Napoleon Bonaparte. He speedily took up the offer to establish friendly relations, and insisted on sealing the alliance with the *fatidra*, a blood oath of brotherhood. The oath was sworn for Britain by Chardenoux and one of his companions, while two young princes and six ministers, including the prime minister Ratala, represented the Merina nation. The ceremony consisted of placing gunpowder, stones, bullets, salt, a gold piece and a ginger root in a bowl. Water was poured into the bowl to cover all the objects it contained. Then:

> *All the participants made a small incision in the stomach to produce a drop of blood which was mixed in with the rest of the ingredients. The point of a spear was plunged into the mixture and everyone held the shaft of the spear in the left hand with the prime minister beating it with a piece of iron in his right hand. All then swore faithful alliance on behalf of their two governments after which they drank a little of the liquid in the bowl. Finally, they placed their hands one on top of the other and the remaining contents of the dish were poured over.*

Radama also agreed to a visit to Mauritius by his ministers, and in addition sent the two royal princes who had taken part in the blood oath to the British island to receive the benefits of a British education. Nor did Radama need much persuasion to allow the British to help modernise his army. He too subscribed to the British point of view that a strong Merina kingdom would finesse any French designs on the island and quickly lead to the happy outcome of 'a single monarch ... in authority over the whole island'; however, his motivation was entirely different. It is quite certain that handing over his crown to the foreigners (the ultimate goal of British diplomacy) figured not at all in his vision of the future. But no matter; for the present the goals of the two parties coincided and all was amity and friendship.

A second British visit to Radama followed on November 17, 1816, led by Farquhar's aide-de-camp, Captain le Sage, and boasting an honour guard of thirty British soldiers, including a company of Bengal sepoys, resplendent in blue trousers and bright red turbans. When the British party reached the lower slopes of the capital, a huge multitude of Radama's soldiery advanced down the hill, dancing and twirling and shooting off their muskets. In response, the newcomers fired off a volley in salutation at each of the many rest stops on the steep approach to the Rova, the royal enclosure, perched at the very top of the mountain, where the king awaited them, seated on his throne. Radama had planned a grandiose ceremony for their arrival, but seeing how drained and sickly his visitors looked, he quickly dispensed with the formalities and sent them to the comfort of their quarters around the palace.

This time the Anglo-Merina treaty of friendship was consummated by the blood oath of King Radama himself, with Captain Le Sage (who had spent fifteen days in a malarial coma after reaching the Merina capital) staggering from his bed of pain to cut his belly and represent the British side of the bargain. Le Sage's continued illness precluded his negotiating many of the points his superiors had hoped he would touch upon with the king, including the vexed question of the slave trade, but when he quit Antananarivo on February 5, 1817, he did leave behind two British non-commissioned officers to begin the military training of King Radama's men.

The task of finalising an official Anglo-Merina treaty, and of including in it Radama's agreement to a suspension of the slave trade, fell first to Thomas Pye, British agent at the coastal port of Tamatave. But ill-health rendered Pye *hors de combat*, and Sergeant James Hastie, who had been tutor to the two Merina princes during their time on Mauritius, was sent in his stead to complete the job and return the princes to their uncle.

Hastie was an Irishman, the son of a miller from Cork, a devout Quaker who had raised his family in an atmosphere of prayer and pacifism. Such peace-loving propensities did not chime well with James Hastie's adventurous soul and, despite possessing an excellent education, he eventually ran off to become a soldier in India. Here he fought with the 56th Regiment during the second Mahratta War of 1803, and was later rewarded with promotion to sergeant, and sent to Mauritius early in 1815. A year later the main roadstead, Port Louis, was engulfed in an inferno that destroyed half the town and threatened to destroy the rest. Only the Governor's House stood between the flames and the rest of the town, and when its roof caught fire most people despaired. But Hastie was undaunted and climbed on to the roof with water on four occasions to douse the flames and save the town from complete destruction. This valiant action brought him to the attention of the Governor, Robert Townsend Farquhar, and it was as a direct consequence of this that the big Irishman was appointed tutor to the two Malagasy princes whom Radama had sent from Madagascar to benefit from a British education.

Once Hastie was established in the Merina capital, British weapons were soon flowing from Her Majesty's ships at anchor in Tamatave Bay through the forested lowlands to Radama's capital of Antananarivo in the central highlands. Under the experienced eyes of the two British non-commissioned officers (now promoted to generals in the Merina army by Radama) the king's troops were rapidly transformed into a first-class military force, equal in both courage and discipline to any European army they might have to face. James Hastie was eventually appointed British agent at Antananarivo, where he spent several years and enjoyed great influence with the Malagasy king:

> *His counsels, which all tended to promote civilisation, had much weight with Radama ... the king gave all the encouragement in his power to [Hastie] and the missionaries, and great advances were made in civilising the kingdom. Infanticide and other cruel customs were abolished and rapid progress was made in the useful arts and in education.*

He was not always successful, however, and on one occasion had to watch in horror as several female servants of the king's sister were put to a medieval-style 'trial by ordeal'. All but one of the poor women failed the test and the 'guilty' were immediately set upon by the executioners, who cut off their ears, noses, arms and legs before casting them to their deaths from a precipitous crag just below the royal Rova. Radama himself seemed unmoved by the atrocity, and Hastie was depressed and dispirited to find that the two royal princes who had returned with him from Mauritius after years of supposedly enlightened education took too obvious a delight in observing the bloody spectacle.

Hastie's 'civilising' efforts in the capital were not entirely disinterested; his presence and usefulness effectively blocked the advance of French designs on Madagascar, thereby greatly helping his own country's interests in the area. He was in great part responsible for the successful conclusion of the 1817 and 1820 treaties between the two nations. In the latter agreement, the British government recognised Madagascar as an independent state, and promised inter alia its continued support for King Radama's regime; in return, the king agreed to abolish slavery throughout his realm in return for recognition of his title of King of Madagascar and a generous annual stipend from London. This included 1,000 dollars in gold, 1,000 dollars in silver, 100 barrels of gunpowder, 100 English muskets with 1,000 flints, 400 soldiers' uniforms, 12 sergeants' swords, 600 pieces of cloth, a full dress uniform for the king, and two fine horses. While slavery was banned in theory, the trade was never completely suppressed and continued in a clandestine manner from many of the smaller ports along the coast, though at a much reduced level.

There was a slight hiccup in Anglo-Merina relations immediately following the signing of the treaty, when the acting Governor of Mauritius, Major-General Gage John Hall, seeing slaves sent just before the treaty was ratified arriving in Mauritius, assumed that the Merina were reneging on their agreement and refused to hand over the necessary compensation without further confirmation from London. When this was reported to Radama, British prestige in Madagascar collapsed, and for a time the saying 'as perfidious as the English' was common in the streets of Antananarivo. But the situation was soon rectified, and the British agreed further concessions, including the provision of British artisans to teach native Malagasy (courtesy of the London Missionary Society, which was only too pleased for the chance to educate *and* proselytise in Radama's domains). Radama also demanded that eight of his men be sent to Mauritius to be trained as a brass band and this unusual request was also acceded to.

On his side, it seems that King Radama genuinely admired British methods of education, government and warfare, and wished to modernise his country along western lines. In later years he became a noted anglophile. During 1820 he encouraged the London Missionary Society to establish churches and later schools in his capital Antananarivo. At first, the Merina believed that the 'Jay-Ho-Vah' advocated by the English priests was the name of the sacred ancestor of the Europeans, and that the *taratsy* they tried to teach – reading and writing – was a superior form of magic.

Despite these misconceptions, over the next few years several thousand students, mainly Merina, were given the rudiments of the 'three Rs'. These practical skills were useful and much sought after, but the other aspect of the missionaries' work, their relgious teaching, was a direct challenge to the traditional Merina culture and to the power of the local fetish priests, and could only bring them into conflict with this influential caucus of native religious leaders. By 1821 the missionaries were using their undoubted influence on the king to insist that their students honour Christmas; twelve months later they were teaching the supremacy of baptism over the traditional ceremony of circumcision and, further, demanding adherence to the European New Year. This latter was a deliberate attempt to undermine the sacred *Fandroana*, the Merina New Year, and only served to stoke the fires of resentment among the traditionalists.

Nevertheless, King Radama continued to indulge the foreign priests. He even permitted nine-year-old twins, the brothers Raombana and Rahaniraka, to take ship for England, where they were to be instructed in western ways under the supervision of the London Missionary Society. So complete was this 'education' that when they returned nine years later, they had forgotten their native tongue and could only converse with their parents and peers via an interpreter.

In addition to spreading the Good News of the Christian message, the missionaries took pains to aid the local Merina economy by setting up craft industries in wood, metal, leather and cotton. So pleased was the king with these advances that, in 1819, Christians were granted a unique status: they would be allowed to stay on the island free of Malagasy laws for a period of ten years. After this time, they would have to submit to the customs of the country or leave Madagascar. Given the Merina's notoriously xenophobic attitude to foreigners, it was an enormous concession and demonstrated the high regard in which the king held the missionaries.

When the London Missionary Society sent James Cameron to Madagascar in 1826, the British were the dominant foreign influence at Imerina and were well pleased with their plan to thwart French colonial designs on the Great Red Island. At 26, Cameron was already a skilled carpenter and weaver, and he soon showed himself a master of many other crafts, helping the Merina to manufacture top-quality bricks, building a reservoir (now known as Lac Anosy) and ensuring royal favour by producing soap entirely from local resources. A few months later the London Missionary Society sent out a printing press, but the English printer who accompanied the machine inconsiderately died from fever almost as soon as his feet had touched the Malagasy shore. Fortunately, the multi-talented Cameron again rose to the challenge: he organised the successful installation and running of the printing press by carefully following the basic printing manual he found in the deceased printer's belongings. This publishing triumph had an enormous effect on the success of the mission. Right at the beginning of their ministry, the protestant missionaries had exerted themselves to learn the local language and they had quickly devised a method of transcribing Malagasy words using the Latin alphabet. Soon, with the help of Cameron's newly arrived printing press, many religious texts and proselytising pamphlets were being published in the Merina tongue. And thanks to the earlier efforts at increasing literacy, the information in the pamphlets was available to a relatively huge number of potential converts. These methods bore fruit quickly, and by 1828 almost half a million Malagasy professed the new foreign faith.

Radama, meanwhile, was using European technology and military discipline to plan further campaigns of conquest. And while the king's relations with the British and French had at times been a copybook example of subtle diplomacy, these methods contrasted sharply with the barbarous tactics of his army, which followed traditional practice in dealing with native enemies – slaying most of the men and carrying the remainder off, along with any women or children, into slavery. The first to feel the might of the Merina army were the neighbouring Betsileo tribe of the southern highlands.

Like the rest of the Malagasy tribes the Betsileo were initially contemptuous of the Merina, regarding their own royal clan as far superior to their upstart neighbours. So exalted were Betsileo royalty that they took the taboo against spilling noble blood on the ground to fantastic extremes. Betsileo aristocrats employed a class of men called *ramanga* ('blue bloods'), whose business it was to 'lick up all the spilt blood of the nobles. Should a noble cut himself, say in cutting his nails or treading on something, the *ramanga* lick up the blood as fast as possible'. The 'blue bloods' also enjoyed the responsibility of eating royal nail parings as soon as they had been cut from fingers or toes. Large nail parings were minced down for ease of swallowing.

*Nobles of high rank hardly go anywhere without these humble attendants, but if it should happen that there are none of them present, the cut nails and spilt blood are carefully collected to be afterwards swallowed by the ramanga.*

For all their pride, the Betsileo were quickly defeated by Radama's better-trained and better-equipped army. Their country was just as rapidly absorbed into a 'Greater Imerina', the defeated menfolk sent captive to the Sakalava tribe on the western coastal fringes, to be sold to European and Arab slavers who took them as far afield as India and America. The Sakalava tribe ('People of the Long Valley') were accomplished slavers and had made themselves powerful by the acquisition of European arms long in advance of the other Malagasy tribes. Together with the Zana Malata, between 1780 and 1820 they had mounted huge slave raids (*razzias*) involving 400–500 outriggers and up to 18,000 warriors on the Comoros islands. These were some of the largest amphibious operations the world has ever seen and they completely overwhelmed the Comorians, whose swords and spears were no match for the European firepower the invaders carried. Such attacks depopulated the Comoros islands to such an extent that the Sakalava eventually reduced the number of boats sent on these raids to around fifty vessels, so as to maintain a 'sustainable yield' of their annual human harvest.

Nor had the highland tribes of Madagascar been immune from Sakalava depredations. During most of the eighteenth century, the People of the Long Valley had used the arms and technology obtained from Arab and European trading to dominate the highland tribes and, except during the reign of King Ralambo, regular Sakalava slaving raids took an especially heavy toll on the Merina people.

Now, with the coming of Radama's organisational genius and the rise of Merina power, the boot was on the other foot. The scene was set for a battle royal to decide which tribe would achieve hegemony over the Great Red Island. The two sides were equally matched in weaponry, but the highland army, with its vastly superior discipline and tactics, held the advantage. In a series of battles in which both sides suffered great losses, Radama gradually reduced the power of the Sakalava and brought most of the tribe under his sway. Now it was the turn of the Sakalava to suffer slaving depredations from the despised Merina, and to pay to their king humiliating quantities of tribute.

With the west coast of Madagascar secured, Radama turned his army about and crossed the central mountains, taking on supplies and additional men as he marched. By 1817, the peoples of the east coast, already aware of the recent fate of the mighty Sakalava and facing an army of 35,000 hardened Merina veterans, submitted with little or no protest. Radama then conquered the entire south-east as far as Tolagnaro. Particularly barren or impenetrable parts of the country and many of the outlying islands escaped conquest, but by his early thirties Radama I had succeeded in bringing the major and more hospitable portions of the country under Merina rule. Despite periodic revolts against his suzerainty (which he put down with horrific retribution, on at least one occasion ordering a rebel leader crucified), Madagascar was his.

He began to title himself not King of the Merina but King of Madagascar, an appellation to which the French – still clinging to their own dreams of conquest and huddled behind the walls of a few coastal bastions – took great exception, lodging a formal protest in 1823. Radama refused even to meet the French mission that had brought the letter of protest, but shortly after sent troops under general Ramananoloma to capture the French bastion of Fort Dauphin. After much loss of life, Ramananoloma took the fortress where, on March 14, 1825, he cut down the French flag and replaced it with Radama's own ensign. While the Merina forces carried off much booty, they did not take their French oppenents prisoner but instead sent them, with every civility, to the French base of Ste Marie.

King Radama had made his point – he alone was the master of Madagascar. Even the European powers' continued presence on the island depended entirely on his good will. Radama's supremacy was unchallenged and he should now have been able to look forward to a long and illustrious reign, but, at the height of his powers, he was struck down – not by an enemy, but by illness and his own weakness for overindulgence.

The king's temperament had often been likened to that of a spoiled child – his response to good news was to dance and sing, while his reaction to misfortune was tears and melancholia. It was the same with his personal relationships: friends were showered with gifts and honours, but his enemies, when in his power, could look for nothing but humiliation and a slow, cruel death. This trait extended to his choice of lifestyle: Radama liked to drink, and he liked women. His ability to consume alcohol was legendary, and he maintained a harem of wives and concubines that would have brought a gleam of envy to the eyes of any Arabian sheik. It was overindulgence in both that eventually carried him off, though it is not possible to say which of his two resulting complaints – cirrhosis of the liver or syphylis – was ultimately responsible for his untimely demise at the relatively young age of thirty-six.

According to his own father's wishes, the throne should have passed to whatever male child had resulted from Radama's union with his (adopted) sister Ranavalona. But either from lack of attention or simple misfortune, Ranavalona had failed to conceive by the king. This was seen by some as a judgement of the gods, for Andrianampoinimerina, Radama's father, had broken with ancient usage by ignoring the Merina's matrilineal traditions and giving the throne to his own son, not to the son of his eldest sister as was the age-old custom. By contrast, the tradition of obedience to the wishes of a dead king (who according to Merina belief was translated to the status of a god on his death) was just as strong, and Ranavalona was seen by many to have a strong claim to the throne, should she ever have the power to prosecute her claim.

With Ranavalona childless, the traditionalist's choice of heir fell on Radama's eldest sister's son, Prince Rakatobe. And he was no friend of the young girl who now found herself a widow, lacking any real power base, and seemingly cast adrift in the ruthless and unforgiving ambience of the Merina court.

# CHAPTER SIX

# Priestess of the Ancestors

The death of a monarch is a dangerous period for any realm, a time of disequilibrium when any or all of the disparate factions held together by the former king may decide that the moment is ripe to make a bid for supreme power. This was especially true in Imerina, where a huge extended family of interconnected kin groups orbited the throne, each with a claim on, or at the very least a desire for, the royal title. Compounding this, the recent empire that Radama's conquests had created seethed with discontent, the numerous ethnic groups itching to revolt from Merina rule at the slightest sign of weakness.

In the face of such dangers, the decision was taken by two favourite officers of the king, Radama's closest confidants, to keep the king's death secret until the legitimately appointed successor, Prince Rakotobe, could be installed securely on the throne. The strategy was a sound one, but one that ultimately played straight into the hands of a single person, Radama's Great Wife, Ranavalona.

According to ancient matrilineal custom, the rightful heir to the Merina throne had long been recognised by traditionalists as

Rakotobe, the eldest son of Radama's eldest sister, and therefore the dead king's 'firstborn' nephew. For many, Andrianampoinimerina's edict, naming any male issue from the union of Ranavalona and Radama heir to the throne, was a blatant sacrilegious attempt to overturn this tradition. But even without a child from this particular union, Radama's own overblown ego would probably have held the kingship from his sister's sons. According to William Ellis, who made several visits to Antananarivo,

> Had Radama lived long enough to have a son grown up to maturity, his ambition would, in all probability, have appointed him as successor to the crown in preference to a sister's child.

But Ranavalona had failed to conceive, and Radama's only other son had died in childhood, 'not without strong suspicions of unfair means having been employed for his destruction by interested parties and near relations'.

One of those 'interested parties' was Ranavalona. Any male child of Radama by another wife was not in her best interests, as it was impossible to predict how he might react to a son from any of his numerous wives. Should the boy prove pleasing in his sight, a favourite, who could predict how the king might arrange his succession? According to the will of Radama's father, Andrianampoinimerina, Ranavalona's children by King Radama had absolute precedence over all others in the race for the crown. But King Radama was a wilful autocrat and as changeable as the wind. A boy child of her own would have secured her position, but King Radama had hardly showered his attentions on Ranavalona, and she had never conceived. This left her in a most dangerous situation.

Without a child of her own she was decidedly vulnerable: as a daughter of the royal bloodline (albeit adopted) any infant she might still produce (by any father) could theoretically be put forward as a legitimate claimant to the throne. Indeed, by virtue of a strange Malagasy custom, any child born to a widow *after* the death of her husband was regarded as the legitimate offspring of her dead spouse, with full rights of inheritance. Ranavalona must have seen that, whoever finally acceded to the kingdom, she would immediately be perceived as a threat. In the ruthless atmosphere of the Merina court such a perception could lead in only one direction – to a swift and untimely death. Her adoption by the royal clan had left her doubly exposed: it had taken her far from her family and she had few blood kin close by to afford her protection. If she wanted to live, Ranavalona had to seize the initiative. Alone. And she had but a single option. She must take the throne herself.

She was not without friends. Unlike the king, who was entranced by western civilisation and the idea of modernising his state, Ranavalona favoured tradition and the ways of her own culture. Nor was she a lover of the western religion, Christianity, preferring the old beliefs and dogma of the *ombiasy* or fetish priests. It was here that she found strong support for her planned coup. The animist priests of the traditional religion had felt themselves increasingly marginalised by King Radama's infatuation with the ministers of the London Missionary Society. They had seen their own positions and power diminish in direct proportion to the increasing influence of the foreign priests and their hateful creed. By contrast, Ranavalona had continued to visit the shrines of the national gods, and to seek counsel from the holy men and oracles of the ancestors. In her, as she knew, the fetish priests saw their own best chance of salvation.

There had been another important effect of the late king's neglect of his Great Wife: she had taken a lover. The object of her affections was Andrianmihaja, a young Merina officer who had recently been promoted to the rank of the sixth honour by King Radama, a reward for his eagerness to fight a duel at the king's insistence. This young brave was an attendant to one of the two officers who were suppressing the knowledge of the king's death and conspiring to put the legal heir, Prince Rakotobe, on the throne. Realising the import of the news, he immediately carried tidings of Radama's death to his lover. It was this prior knowledge, and this alone, that gave Ranavalona the time she needed to put her coup into action.

What happened next occurred with such speed and precision that it is hard not to suspect a high degree of forward planning. As soon as Radama's Great Wife knew of her husband's demise she summoned to her presence, in the deepest secrecy, two colonels of the Merina army. These men hailed from her own home village and were probably at least loosely related to Ranavalona. Swiftly, she informed them of the king's death and of her intention to seize the throne herself. As the cicadas and whistling frogs threw their calls out into the humid night, she offered position and fortune in return for their loyalty and aid: she would load them with slaves, money and land, secure for them the highest rank in the army, and grant them *tsy maty manota*, a privilege that guaranteed the holder exemption from execution, no matter how heinous the offence. Without hesitation, both men swore to support her to the death; no idle oath, for a hideous end would undoubtedly be their fate, and that of Ranavalona, should the putsch fail.

As an earnest of their good faith, the two officers immediately conveyed Ranavalona and a close female friend (another of Radama's twelve senior wives) to a place of safety, concealing them in a private house a little way from the palace. They then hurried to the sleeping quarters of the chief priests and judges of the capital, who unanimously gave their support to the 'queen's' accession. Now more confident of success, the pair roused the army divisions under their direct command and returned to the palace. So swiftly and secretly had these measures been taken that General Rafozehana, the senior officer in the capital and a known supporter of Prince Rakotobe, was still utterly unaware that anything untoward was afoot. He was summoned to the palace on a pretext, and presented with what amounted to a fait accompli: Ranavalona would be proclaimed Queen of Madagascar within the hour – was he for or against her accession? Bravely, he tried to buy time, requesting a day's delay while he mustered his own troops. His request was denied, and the question repeated, with an insistence that he must immediately declare for or against. The conspirators would brook no delay.

There is little doubt that, had he been able to escape the confines of the palace, the general planned to suppress Ranavalona's revolution and install the rightful heir on the throne. But the gates of the palace were closed and barred, and he was surrounded by desperate men whose lives were now firmly bound to the success of the coup. To support Prince Rakotobe meant certain, instant death. Without hesitation, General Rafozehana stepped forward, and 'saved himself by becoming a zealous and eloquent partisan of the queen'.

The palace was now secure, the officer commanding the capital had vouchsafed his support, and the judges and fetish priests were in attendance as guarantors of the goodwill of the gods and ancestral spirits. But when the gods' approval was announced to the assembled troops, matters began to go awry. Four officers of the Tsindranolahy (the king's bodyguard) refused to accept Ranavalona's accession, stating firmly that:

> they could not, whatever the consequences, conceal the fact that the late King had named Rakotobe and Raketaka [Radama's own daughter] as the party to succeed him.
>
> They had scarcely given this proof of fidelity to their late sovereign than twenty or thirty spears were plunged into them by the bystanders, and they perished on the spot.

There were no more protests. The order was given to fire the palace cannon and amid great tumult and acclamation Ranavalona was proclaimed Queen of Madagascar. It was the morning of August 1, 1828.

The bloodbath began soon after. Time had not healed the new queen's ancient resentment for Radama's execution of her kinfolk; the blood feud was a commonplace of Merina life and Ranavalona was not immune to its sanguinary call. Besides, Malagasy history showed clearly that only a fool allowed rival claimants to survive.

Immediately after the coup Prince Rakotobe had been apprehended as he attempted to escape the capital. He was kept in chains, and over the next few days moved from one village to another, perhaps as a precaution against a rescue attempt by his supporters, while Ranavalona decided his fate. Thankfully, given the atrocities that were to mark the new queen's rule, his end was swift – on her orders, the rightful heir to the Merina kingdom was speared to death in a small village about twenty miles from the capital. At the same time, Rakotobe's father, then serving as governor of the port of Tamatave, was summoned to the capital by Ranavalona. When he obeyed her call, he was immediately declared guilty of leaving his post, a capital offence. There was no appeal against Ranavalona's revenge, and he too was speared to death, at Ambatomanga on October 6. His wife Rabodosahondro, Prince Rakotobe's mother and the sister of King Radama, was also placed under arrest. She escaped the spear; in deference to the taboo that forbade the shedding of royal female blood, Ranavalona ordered her sister-in-law starved to death. Implacably, the new queen's vengeance moved back along the royal bloodline, bringing death in her wake. King Radama's mother suffered the same fate as her daughter; Ratafika, the last surviving brother, was captured and also starved to death. The late king's only surviving maternal uncle, Adrianilana, was taken by the queen's men and executed at the same time. Another noble, Radama's cousin, was treacherously slain by his second-in-command.

Anyone remotely linked to the royal family appears to have been executed: some strangled, some drowned or 'taborined', a dreadful torture of the genitals. Others were thrown to their deaths from the heights of Ambohipoptsy, the sheer rock face close to the capital reserved for the execution of criminals. Perfumed and adorned in her finery, Ranavalona watched many of these executions from the verandah of her palace, and betrayed not the slightest pity for the victims. Later commentators have claimed that this was because she saw herself as the true heir of both Andrianampoinimerina and King Radama, and so viewed any conspiracy against herself as a 'dynastic crime' that threatened to wreck the kingdom that both her great predecessors had striven to gain at such a huge cost in blood and effort. This may well be a partial explanation of the ruthless savagery she displayed in disposing of her rivals, but the remainder of her reign points clearly to a sanguinary disposition that enjoyed the suffering of others as an end in itself. Whatever the motivation, the executions served their purpose well. As the wave of annihilation spread outwards from Ranavalona's central dominating figure, the royal line of King Radama simply ceased to exist.

There was one exception. For some reason, the new queen saw fit to spare Radama's only surviving child, the daughter of Salima, the 'black and beautiful' princess of the coastal Sakalava tribe, Radama's favourite and the only woman the king seems to have truly loved. From a matrilineal point of view, the girl was of the Sakalava bloodline, and it is this – perhaps – that saved her. There may also have been a political motive for Ranavalona's apparent kindness. The Sakalava were a large, proud and warlike people, their land and cities constantly bubbling with barely suppressed revolt. Sparing Salima and her daughter would have flattered and placated the Sakalava, and may simply have been an expedient ploy for heading off potential rebellion following Radama's death.

A few people actively escaped Ranavalona's wrath. One potential rival, Ramanetaka, took ship for the Comoros Islands and settled on Mohilla. Another, Andriantsolo, fled to the northwest and lived in exile on one of the small islets off the coast. But though alive, all those who survived were scattered and powerless, and constituted no great threat to the queen's continued rule.

Certainly, none remained to impede her formal, and very public, installation as queen that occurred soon after at Andouale, the forum and chief market of Antananarivo.

On the morning of the ceremony, on June 12, 1829, another much more secret ritual had been performed. Ranavalona had risen early to bathe, after which she was attended by Ranour, known as the 'Mother of the Blacks'. Kneeling before her, Ranour had daubed the queen's breasts and pudendum with the still-warm blood of a freshly sacrificed bull. Then, taking a bowl containing a paste made from holy water and the dust of sacred tombs, she painted a bright stripe across Ranavalona's forehead. The old negress enclosed her mistress, thus sanctified with the twin symbols of life and death, in a protective triple circle, invoking the sacred twenty-one syllables as she completed her work.

All around the queen the princesses of the blood bustled to and fro, some burning branches of the aromatic 'Fairy Tree' and hanging the queen's vestments in the purifying flames. Others sang charms against sorcerers and witchcraft, while the remainder sprinkled holy water over the bells, amulets, talismans and other fetishes that Ranavalona must, by tradition, carry with her. The queen meanwhile was being dressed in her most prestigious robes and finery. On her head was a fabulous crown of gold, pearls and branched coral, dressed with five sparrowhawk plumes and four curved crocodile teeth. In contrast to the essentially African nature of the ceremony, and reflecting the love–hate, almost schizoid relationship that existed between the Merina and the Europeans, Ranavalona would go to her 'coronation' dressed in the finest French fashions: over a bodice of white silk, ordered from Mauritius, she put on a magnificent robe of red velour, embroidered with gold, and from her shoulders there hung an endless canopy of white satin, shot through with gold thread, fashioned by the Creole couturiers of Ile Bourbon, its design based on the costume of the Empress Josephine of France. There could be no more telling metaphor for the whole of Merina society: the haute couture of France covering breasts stained with sacrificial blood.

Her toilet complete, the palace women raised the slight figure of the queen onto the shoulders of the tallest of her guards, for it was taboo for the sovereign's feet to touch the earth, nor was it permitted that any of her subjects should look down upon her. Carrying her lightly down the palace stairs, he placed her on a sumptuous float, drawn by eight 'sparrowhawks', Merina cadets chosen by Ranavalona for their great beauty and, if the rumours were true, much else besides. To a thunderous cannonade, the palanquin moved slowly off, surrounded by five uniformed generals, sabres drawn, and accompanied by two gigantic red parasols, a Malagasy symbol of royalty. Behind them, in ranks of ten, two hundred white-clad female singers followed the procession, while the royal band played, incongruously, European military music: 'L'air de la Reine' and 'La Complainte de Marlborough'. With great pomp the procession left the palace and made its slow way downhill to Andouale, the forum and main market of Antananarivo where a great multitude, more than 100,000 people, were assembled. Massed on the verandahs of every available house, perched on walls, squeezed between the terraced tombs of the cemetery and crammed together on the natural amphitheatre of rocks that climbed in a great semicircle towards the Royal City, towering above, this huge throng of bustling, babbling humanity impatiently awaited the arrival of their new sovereign.

Near the centre of Andouale a large, oddly shaped stone had been set up long ago, revered by all the Merina people, and believed by them to be a conduit between this world and the spirits of the deified and powerful former rulers of the kingdom. Ranavalona's eight sparrowhawks brought her litter to a halt before this sacred stone. A great silence fell on the huge crowd, and the air was suddenly alive with numinous expectation. Shaded by an immense parasol, the diminutive figure of the queen slowly stepped down, placing both her feet on this object of universal veneration. Only by contact with the sacred stone could the essential virtue, the spirit of royalty, be transmitted to this new claimant to the Merina throne, legitimating her rule.

Ranavalona's five generals, dressed in richly brocaded uniforms, removed their tricorn hats and surrounded the sacred spot, swords at the ready. For a long moment Ranavalona stood erect on the revered menhir, alone and silent, surveying her subjects. Then she raised the magic sceptre she held in her right hand and, her voice shaking with emotion, demanded of the crowd their acceptance of her rule:

'You, *Izao ambany*, Those Beneath the Sky! Am I consecrated?'

Her five generals responded for the crowd. Shaking their hats and brandishing their swords skyward, they cried in unison: 'Majesty, true heart, strong soul, you are consecrated, consecrated, consecrated!'

At these words the people erupted in a frenzy of delight: 'Houb! Houb! Houb! Live forever Ranavalona-Manjaka! Ranavalona-Majesty, live eternally!'

Amid the noise and clamour, Ranavalona took from under their covering of red silk the wooden images of Fataka and Manjakatsir, the two great tutelary deities of the kingdom. Holding them aloft in the sudden silence, she addressed them reverently: 'I have received you from my ancestors. I put my trust in you. Therefore support me.'

Protected now by the spirits of dead monarchs and the gods, she returned the idols to their keepers, who placed them once again beneath their scarlet covers.

With the main part of the ceremony completed, the newly consecrated ruler was carried to a wide, crimson-covered platform on which stood an enormous throne of purple and gold. Ranged around her were the members of her court: on her left the secretary of state, Renihar, and to her right Andrianmihaja, her prime minister and her lover. Behind the princes of the blood, the marshals and generals, stood the governors of the provinces and behind them the chiefs of the tributary states, all wearing their different national costumes, and each ranked according to his status and importance. The Sultan of Oman and ruler of the Comores islands had both sent delegates to the ceremony, while the ambassador of the Sultan of Zanzibar, a huge figure swathed in silk and sparkling with diamonds, had arrived with gifts of fine pearls, cloves and horses to request the hand of the new queen for his master. The offer also included 2,000 armed men to fight for the new regime. Ranavalona was to turn down this alliance, though she took pains not to offend its proposer. It was an early indication of a determination that remained unshaken throughout her long reign – she would rule alone, beholden to none.

As if to emphasise this steadfast resolve, she rose from her throne again to address her people. The Great God, she announced, and all the lesser gods and goddesses, had given this land to her ancestors, as had the spirits of the wind, forest, stones and waters. And the ancestors had bequeathed their rule to Andrianampoinimerina, who in the course of time had granted it to King Radama, on the express condition that he bequeathed it in turn to her. 'Is this not so?'

'It is so! It is so!' came the enthusiastic response from 100,000 throats. Whether this was true or not was immaterial to the populace. Ranavalona had stood on the sacred stone; her rivals were dead or scattered. What more proof was needed of the will of the gods?

'Never say,' she continued, raising her sceptre to the sky, 'she is only a feeble and ignorant woman, how can she rule such a vast empire? I *will* rule here, to the good fortune of my people and the glory of my name! I will worship no gods but those of my ancestors. The ocean shall be the boundary of my realm, and I will not cede the thickness of one hair of my realm!' So saying, she let her sceptre fall, and to tumultuous acclamation took her seat again on the golden throne.

It fell to Minister of State Renihar to respond. With many flamboyant gestures he called on the people to witness the queen's consecration and her promises. And he assured the assembled Merina elite, and the tributary states, of the protection of the new monarch, 'Priestess of the Ancestors' and 'Eye-of-God on Earth'. Then, turning to his sovereign, he held out to Ranavalona a solitary coin, a single spanish *piastre*, the symbolic offering by which the common people traditionally 'bought' from their ruler 'the right to life'. She took the proffered coin in dignified silence, and with its acceptance the ceremony of accession was complete. It remained only for the assembled dignitaries – princes, officers, ambassadors, delegates and European guests – to approach the throne in due order, each according to rank and nation, and to offer their submission or congratulations to the Great Glory as they departed Andouale for their lodgings in the capital.

It was done. The successful completion of this ritual had been vital to Ranavalona's long-term security, for it carried as much psychological and spiritual authority for the Merina people as a Christian coronation in a great abbey might have for Europeans. Ranavalona I was undisputed Queen of the Imerina, and of much of Madagascar besides.

The success of Ranavalona's coup brought a seismic shift both within Madagascar society and in the Great Red Island's relations with the rest of the world. Almost as soon as she had ascended the throne, the new queen took care to reassure the Europeans of her firm intention to follow Radama's policy in ruling the country. But from the start a reaction against modernisation began to gain momentum.

King Radama's closeness to the British had extended to allowing the accredited agent of that nation, his 'good friend' James Hastie, to reside in the capital. Hastie had died at Antananarivo some two years earlier and the British had been slow in sending a replacement. By coincidence, the new British agent, Mr Lyall, had arrived in the Malagasy capital on August 1, the very day that the Ranavalona faction had gained the ascendancy. Like everyone else in Madagascar, he had been unaware of King Radama's demise until Ranavalona's plot had succeeded, and he was then kept waiting several weeks for an opportunity to present his credentials to the new monarch. He and his family were held in this diplomatic limbo until November 29, when a message was received from the queen stating that she would repudiate King Radama's Anglo-Malagasy treaties, and that she would not recognise Mr Lyall as the British agent in her country. The message acknowledged that this action would mean the subsidy provided by the British would be lost, but that in consequence it was the queen's intention to revive the slave trade. It was evident that not only was King Radama's family to be destroyed by the new queen, Ranavalona was grimly intent on extinguishing her husband's political legacy also.

There is little doubt that this blunt missive to the hated foreigner greatly pleased the fetish priests and those other adherents whose backing had been so crucial during the early stages of her coup. But it was also designed to garner additional support from within the lower orders of Merina society. In times past (that is, before King Radama and his treaties with the British), the buying and selling of slaves had enriched almost everyone. The predatory military expeditions that were a way of life for the Merina had garnered a bountiful human harvest each dry season, and kept the wheels of the economy well greased. Radama's treaties had compensated the king for loss of revenue, but the benefits of British largesse had hardly trickled down to the ordinary citizen. Repudiating the ban on slave trading was therefore an immensely popular move, equivalent perhaps to a modern-day cut in income tax: it promised increased prosperity and a buoyant economy.

It soon became apparent that Ranavalona's reign would not herald a time of peace and joy for all the people of Madagascar. She made it plain from the beginning that her conception of royalty was the eastern model of absolute despotism. Society was a pyramid, at the base of which were the mass of common people, who could command no one and who, indeed, must even buy the right to life from their sovereign. Above the commoners were increasingly smaller classes who had the privilege of commanding obedience from those below them, but who likewise were subordinate to the higher ranks of the social pyramid. And at the very summit stood the queen, whose authority was above all challenge, from whom all position and privilege were derived, and who claimed the unquestioning obedience of every member of society. Her will was law, she was accountable to no one and bound to no superior allegiance than that of the ancestors and tribal gods.

This system was formalised in a rigid caste system of anything up to eleven grades (the number varied during different reigns). At the pinnacle, in a caste of one, was the monarch. Below this most exalted level, the second caste was composed of the king or queen's family. The nobles (*andriana*), of which there were many, were divided into around six separate groupings, all intensely jealous of their rank and privileges. Below these were the *folovohitra* (people of the ten villages), the common people descended from the original ten villages of central Imerina, every-one from professional people, through traders and merchants, to the peasantry. The *mainty* (blacks) were a caste of freed slaves and royal servants, who ranked above the lowest social strata, the *andevo* or slave caste, with white slaves positioned above their dark-skinned brothers, presumably on the basis of their rarity.

Whether it was the absolute autocratic power that she now wielded or the emotional satisfaction she obtained from the extinguishing of King Radama's line, the new queen rapidly displayed a disquieting taste for blood. The society of which she found herself the head was hardly noted for its pacifism, but she quickly brought the practice of barbaric rites to new heights of coarseness and savagery. Under Ranavalona, torture, crucifixion and beheadings became common sights. Brigands, runaway slaves, rebels and anyone suspected of traitorous leanings might be flayed alive, or sawn in half, or have their testicles slowly crushed in the horrendous *sakina*. Others might be bound, then sewn into buffalo hides, with only their heads protruding, and hung up on poles and left to die slowly from the sun, starvation and dehydration. For the worst offences, the victims would be fastened to wooden stakes in specially dug waist-high pits, into which huge cauldrons of boiling water were poured, to cook the bodies from the waist down while leaving the upper part of the torso and the head intact and the sufferer only too conscious of their fate.

For many of these unfortunate victims, their only error was to fail a judicial process known as the *tanguena*. This was a mockery of a trial, more akin to the 'ordeal' of the European Middle Ages, in which guilt or innocence depended on the accused's response to a particularly virulent plant poison, extracted from the seed of the tanguena plant, a species of local shrub. The test was used to determine the truth only in particularly heinous offences, such as suspected treason. Ideally, the subject was kept without food for a full day before being fed a specially prepared 'meal', consisting of rice, three pieces of chicken skin, and the crushed or scraped kernel from the tanguena bush. Copious amounts of water were then forced on the suspect to induce vomiting – for it was in the manner in which regurgitation occurred that truth or innocence was determined. If all three pieces of chicken skin were brought up, the suspect was deemed innocent and immediately released; but should two or fewer pieces appear, the case against him or her was considered proven, and the miscreant was hauled away for immediate execution (though usually not before some form of additional torture, such as limb amputation or flaying, had taken place). A deposit of twenty-eight dollars was normally paid by the person who had brought the accusation; if the accused was found guilty, this money was returned. But should the regurgitation prove the suspect innocent, the deposit was split evenly between the accuser, the accused and the crown. In some more serious cases, if the suspect were shown to be innocent, the accuser might be condemned to death in the same manner in which the suspect would have died, had his or her guilt been proved.

Ranavalona did not invent the *tanguena*: the trial by ordeal was a traditional test, sanctioned by custom. It was flourishing in King Radama's time, in 1817, when the British agent James Hastie arrived at Antananarivo. Even worse was another practice current at that time, in which a suspect was 'tried' by progressive amputation. First the fingers were cut off one at a time, then the hands, feet, and finally the limbs. As each bodily part was severed, the suspect was invited to confess. If he admitted his guilt, he was instantly executed; if he refused, more limbs were removed until death ensued. It was a method that ensured a conviction rate of one hundred per cent. Under pressure from Hastie, King Radama had refused to ban the *tanguena*, but had agreed to allow dogs to deputise for the human participants in the ordeal. As with most of her husband's commands, Ranavalona revoked this humane decision on his death, and spent her time on the throne enthusiastically promoting its use on human suspects. It has been estimated that several thousand of the queen's subjects perished by the *tanguena*. Given the irrational nature of the 'evidence', it is likely that the majority of them were innocent.

Mr Lyall doggedly remained in the capital while the country moved rapidly away from its former modernising, pro-British stance. He was undoubtedly hoping for a change of attitude in the queen, but his presence was all but ignored by Ranavalona's officials. Matters worsened rapidly until March 29 the following year, when a large mob of citizens, carrying snakes in their hands, chanting loudly and led by fetish priests of the Ramahavaly idol, surrounded Lyall's house and forced him and his sons to remove themselves to the village of Ambhipeno, about six miles distant from the capital. They were followed a few days later by the rest of his family, and within a month the whole group had been transported to the port of Tamatave, where they took ship for the safety of Mauritius. In all this Ranavalona did nothing to help the Europeans and it can hardly be doubted that the whole exercise was carried out under her direction. British influence at the Merina court, which had lasted over eleven years, was now effectively at an end.

The British, with a burgeoning empire and unshakeable sense of their own importance in the world, were hardly likely to take this insult lying down. Nor were the French, who several years before had protested at King Radama's assumption of the title of King of Madagascar (rather than King of the Merina). The French laid claim to those eastern parts of Madagascar that they had colonised under Jacques de Pronis in 1643, and they were unlikely to cede such valuable territory to anyone without a fight. There was no question in Ranavalona's mind: sooner or later the hated Europeans would be back in force.

Until then the guardians of the ancestral ways were in the ascendancy, xenophobia was rife in the streets of Antananarivo, and a violent wave of conservative reaction against western ways swept the capital. This political reality posed a serious and very real problem in the queen's personal life. In the immediate aftermath of the revolution, Ranavalona's gratitude to Andrianmihaja had known no bounds. He was her lover, and the officer whose information on King Radama's death had been so vital to the success of her coup. At her express command, he had been raised to unheard-of heights of power and influence: chosen as the queen's personal adviser and prime minister, he had also been elevated to the rank of commander in chief of the army. His liaison with King Radama's Great Wife, once so secret, now became common knowledge and he was looked on by one and all as the queen's husband, in all but name.

Such a meteoric rise in fortune could only stimulate the jealousy and hatred of Andrianmihaja's erstwhile superiors. A cabal formed, headed by three brothers, Rainiharo, Rainijohary and Rainiseheno, dedicated to the removal of the queen's favourite. This was natural enough – such conspiracies were commonplace at the Merina court, and as such it posed no difficulty to the new queen. But the problem was much worse than simple intrigue and collusion among courtiers. Andrianmihaja was a known admirer of European ways and very appreciative of British organisational ability. Worse, he made no secret of his sympathies. This newly forbidden attitude could not easily be smoothed over and it made him vulnerable. In the febrile xenophobic atmosphere of the palace, his overtly 'westernising' attitude was an immediate target for attack by the forces of reaction, especially from the priests of the old gods.

Compounding this, his amorous connection to the queen, and his sudden rise to power through her, threatened the new ruler with guilt by association. Any suspicion that Ranavalona harboured Europhile inclinations would spell disaster for her reign; it threatened to remove the support and power on which the security of her rule depended.

Ranavalona's response to this problem revealed the depths of her superstition, and her susceptibility to the pronouncements of the fetish priests. It also laid bare a terrifying jealousy and ruthlessness when she felt herself betrayed. The brothers' triumvirate constantly attacked Andrianmihaja's loyalty, and they prevailed on the priesthood to make similar accusations against the queen's 'husband'. Such accusations of treason could best be disproved by the *tanguena* ordeal. But it seems that Ranavalona's affection for Andrianmihaja remained undimmed, and she would not allow him to face the fatal test again (on her accession, all officers in attendance on the queen had been forced to undergo the *tanguena* ordeal, as a precaution against witchcraft and treason). Instead, Andrianmihaja was refused entry to the queen's presence and dismissed from court. This, it appears, was Ranavalona's attempt to save the man she loved, and at the same time to demonstrate to those about her that she remained true to the old traditions of her country. Andrianmihaja might be disgraced, she might forbid him the intimacy he formerly enjoyed, but the man to whom she most owed her throne was at least alive.

And so he might have remained, had he been content for a while to live the celibate life of a discarded paramour. The world of the court was one of constantly changing loyalties and status, and it is possible that Ranavalona planned to bring her lover back to the palace just as soon as circumstances permitted. But it was not to be. Within weeks, word was brought to the queen of Andrianmihaja's liaison with a young princess of the blood royal.

This news changed everything. While the possibility of his treason might be borne with equanimity, the knowledge of Andrianmihaja's amourette, of his physical betrayal with another woman, turned Ranavalona's heart to stone, and produced the response for which the leaders of reaction had until now laboured in vain. The accusation of treason was reinstated, and his attendance at the *tanguena* ordeal commanded by the queen herself.

To general consternation, Andrianmihaja refused to submit to the *tanguena*. It was a response almost without precedent, for there could be but one outcome to his open defiance of the monarch's will. Why he chose this fatal course is a mystery. It is possible that he made his stand in order to put the queen, his 'wife', to a test of his own devising – to divine the true feelings of this woman whom he had helped bring to the throne. It may be that Andrianmihaja loved her more deeply than Ranavalona knew, and that his rejection, his dismissal from court and the queen's affections, had so reduced his spirits that he felt the risk worth taking. Would her love for him triumph over her lust for power? How would she choose?

Given Ranavalona's ruthless temperament, it was a high-risk strategy. And it failed utterly. If she hoped to maintain her grip on the throne Ranavalona simply could not afford to allow such open defiance of her will. When it came to a choice, there could be but one decision. At the queen's royal command, Andrianmihaja was sentenced to die.

By all accounts the queen's 'husband' took the news with remarkable sangfroid; an indication, perhaps of his low state of mind. Even when the fatal moment arrived and the executioner entered his presence carrying the silver spear, *tsitialaingia*, tied with royal purple, he did not lose his equanimity. The execution 'was carried out in his own residence – Andrianmihaja with cool self-possession directing his executioner with his own fingers to the exact spot where to plunge the knife in his throat'. Before he died he is said to have given his assassin a Spanish *piastre*, saying: 'Take this to the queen. Tell her it is the price of my blood.' Then, even as the executioner's blow struck home, he cried: 'Glory to Ranavalona-Manjaka, sovereign of heaven and earth. Live forever without misfortune!' His body was treated with all respect: he was buried at Namehana, 'and his memory long after haunted the miserable queen in visions at night.'

But it was not in the queen's nature to grieve for long. Despite her affection for the dead man, Andrianmihaja was soon replaced in her amours by the three brothers who had schemed so hard to bring about his downfall. They swiftly came to share her bed and her affections, and in addition to replacing the unfortunate Andrianmihaja as 'husband' of the queen, they were each allotted a portion of his honours. Rainiharo became commander in chief of the army, Rainijohary the chief officer of the palace, and Rainiseheno was granted a position as one of the country's principal judges (he died soon after and so was unable to take advantage of either the carnal or the governmental honours that the queen bestowed on his two siblings).

If she did not long lament her lost lover, ancient tradition demanded a twelve-month mourning period for a dead monarch. Ranavalona cut this period to ten months, which some saw as an oblique criticism of Radama's rule. But Ranavalona was well aware that the king was fondly remembered by his people, and that her own legitimacy rested, at least in part, on her fulfilling the traditional funeral rites of the dead monarch. She commanded, on pain of death, that all ranks, from the nobles to the common people, should shave their hair in token of mourning, and reshave their heads regularly for at least three months. Only the twelve 'royal wives' and the princes and princesses of the blood were exempt from this duty. The professional mourners were also allowed to keep their tresses, but only so that they could better tear out their hair in an ecstasy of grief during the actual funeral.

All pleasures were likewise proscribed: dancing, bathing, clapping the hands, riding in a palanquin, playing a musical instrument, sleeping on a mattress, regarding one's face in a mirror – all were forbidden, with perpetual slavery the fate of those found guilty of breaking the taboos. With a fine touch of irony (given the probable cause of the king's demise), the guild of prostitutes was allowed to ply its trade without restriction, but only on the firm understanding that half the proceeds of their work were handed over to the shade of the dead king, and that they agreed to dance and sing in commemoration of the royal burial.

After the body of Radama was washed, it was wrapped in a shroud of the traditional *simbu* or toga, of red silk. Great numbers of *simbu* were used, the amount being determined by the status of the deceased. Radama's body was encased in several hundred *simbu* before being placed on an ornate wooden table, under a canopy of red silk. Scores of slaves were set around the coffin, each armed with a long-handled fan, with which they were charged to keep the flies from the corpse. As the lying in state would last for weeks, and the flies gave no respite by night or day, squads of slaves were delegated to relieve each other so that the insects could be driven off round the clock. On all sides, hundreds of the late king's young concubines sat and mourned, keening out a high-pitched dirge as they rocked and swayed in their misery. Beyond them, four ranks of soldiers stood guard, their muskets reversed as a sign of mourning.

In combination with these traditional rites, Ranavalona was determined that the obsequies of her dead husband would be remembered forever at Imerina. Despite her ardent xenophobia, it seems that she had been impressed by the European reproductions that had been brought to the capital by travellers showing the interments of the British king, George III, and of France's Louis XV. She decided that the funeral of Madagascar's king, the Malagasy Napoleon, would be no less magnificent in its pomp and ostentation.

A huge catafalque was constructed to take the body of the king, hung with purple and scarlet silk, festooned with feathers and sparkling with a multitude of mirrors, requisitioned from all around the capital. Two staircases, bordered with candelabra of pure silver, led to a platform on which the king's body lay, enclosed in its innumerable layers of silk, like some grotesque chrysalis of death. Below the catafalque, the chief mourners, the royal family, gave voice to their woe. All except the queen: as the symbolic 'light incarnate', she was not allowed to come near a cadaver, nor to cry over a body that the Great Darkness had taken.

Throughout the days that the corpse lay in state there came an endless procession of envoys from all parts of the country and from all the various castes of Merina society, and with them long trains of servants and slaves, bringing gifts of condolence from themselves and from those in whose name they had been sent. Each donation was collected by the close relations of the king, who used them to help defray the huge cost of the royal funeral. While all this was going on, at one side of the royal courtyard Ranavalona's silversmiths were hard at work constructing an enormous, ornate coffin for her dead spouse. On the other side of the plaza a stone-built mausoleum was rising from the ground, built four square, with half the structure beneath the earth and, rising above it, a heavy roof constructed in the form of a terrace.

Once the tomb was completed it was filled with the king's most treasured possessions, most of them gifts from European ambassadors and friends: a huge four-poster bed hung with scarlet curtains, a chaise longue, trunks and cases stuffed with the king's 79 feathered and tricorn hats, 155 magnificent military uniforms, 171 pairs of brocaded trousers, 95 waistcoats of various styles and colours, cravats, gloves, scarves, snuffboxes, writing cases, rifles, swords, Chinese vases, silver plate, boxes of music, portraits of George IV, Frederick the Great, Napoleon and Louis XIII, and, in pride of place, an enormous golden escutcheon, bearing the coat of arms of George IV of England and inscribed 'To My brother Radama'.

Alongside these tokens of western civilisation, golden chains, bracelets, hairpieces and earrings without number were carried into the king's last resting place, together with belts of alligator teeth and other outlandish charms and talismans. When all was complete, on the terrace of the mausoleum a small wooden cabin was built, a copy of the traditional huts of the Malagasy peasant, or at least so it seemed from the outside. Within, Ranavalona caused it to be fitted out with all the accoutrements of a Paris boudoir, furnished with two easy chairs and a small pedestal table on which was placed a carafe of water, a bottle of sweet wine and two glasses. Here, the shade of Radama could visit, and drink and converse with the spirit of his old friend, the Irishman Hastie, who had died in the capital two years earlier. It was a gesture that revealed Ranavalona's devotion to the dead king, despite his own lack of affection towards his Great Royal Wife.

Twelve days were needed to complete these funeral arrangements. At dawn the next day, batteries of cannon kept up a continuous fusillade as the people gathered to bury their king. To the strains of 'March of the Grenadiers' and 'La Complainte de Marlborough', six of Radama's favourite horses, the gift of Robert Farquhar, Governor of Mauritius, were sacrificed on the threshold of the mausoleum. Twelve white heifers, representing Radama's twelve wives, were also immolated, recalling an earlier time when the Merina monarch's wives were expected to die alongside him and accompany their king to the land of the spirits.

At midday, sixty high-ranking military men, generals or marshals of the Merina army, marched through the four lines of soldiers surrounding the catafalque and carried the gigantic, silk-covered remains of Radama to his tomb. He was laid on the giant four-poster, the silk curtains were closed, and around the bed were hung, as sentinels, the portraits of the foreign kings. Then thirty princes of the blood rolled the stone door of the tomb closed, leaving only the inscription, written in Malagasy, in Latin text:

Antananarivo, 1st August 1828
RADAMA MANJAKA
Sovereign of the Great Island
Without Equal Among Its Kings

The rites and ceremonies had now all been completed: King Radama was buried; Ranavalona's dead husband had been laid to rest in his tomb with the honours and devotions that would ensure his quiet rest. And she had been crowned queen with all due pomp, and with the open approval of the gods and the people. But there was only a short time to enjoy the fruits of her realm. In October of the same year, the French returned, in strength, to press their claims on her territory.

# CHAPTER SEVEN

# La Visite Amicale

The French colonists on the island of Reunion had been pressing their home government to mount an expedition against Madagascar since the time of King Radama's death. However, questions of cost were uppermost in the French administration's thoughts and they were not minded to permit any adventure until, in the first month of 1829, the intercession of the French King Charles X changed the situation completely. The garrisons on the French possessions of Reunion and Ile Ste Marie (the latter lying just off the Madagascan west coast) were due to be relieved at the end of the year. At the suggestion of the minister of marine, the king proposed that these relief forces, plus several companies of Yolof troops from the French Senegal, should not await the close of 1829, but set sail for the Indian Ocean immediately. There, they could combine with the French forces presently on Reunion and Ste Marie and together make *une visite amicale* to the Great Red Island to present the new queen with their country's compliments and their demands.

In early June, a French squadron under the command of *capitaine de vaisseau* Gourbeyre assembled at Port St Denis, Reunion. The flotilla comprised six vessels, with the original four ships from France (the frigate *Terpsichore*, the corvette *La Nievre*, the gabare *La Chevrette* and a transport *L'Infatigable*) being augmented by a despatch boat *Colibri* and a second transport *Madagascar*. The ships carried infantry, gunners and military labourers for building the fortifications that the French intended to raise on 'their' Malagasy soil. Captain Gourbeyre was charged with delivering lavish presents to Her Majesty Ranavalona, 'Queen of the Hova' (the French were adamant that the title Queen of Madagascar be denied the new monarch). At the same time he was also required to place before Her Majesty a demand that she recognise French rights 'over the greatest portion of the eastern coast'. Being well aware of the eastern practice of simply ignoring, rather than refusing, the demands of other powers, the good captain was ordered to inform the queen that should no favourable answer be given by her after eight days, French rights would be imposed by force of arms. Full of resolve, the French flotilla raised anchor and set sail for Madagascar.

They arrived on July 9 in the roadstead off the town of Tamatave, to discover that the Merina garrison was already refurbishing its defences. The *visite amicale* was looking increasingly shaky, and Captain Gourbeyre decided against sending a delegation to the queen – the hostile intentions of the populace were already clear, and he feared for the life of anyone foolhardy enough to make the journey to her highland capital. Instead, he made do with a long letter to Her Majesty Ranavalona stating the demands of the French government and allowing 20 days for a response. With the ultimatum entrusted to a native runner, the French sailed for a small outpost, long abandoned, at Tintingue, where they constructed a stout bastion armed with eight cannon. As they worked, the Merina forces were busily engaged in building an equally impressive fortification at nearby Larée Point. The omens did not appear favourable for a peaceful settlement to the differences between the two nations.

The October 10 deadline came and passed with no word from Ranavalona. The French returned to Tanatave where, with due formality, Captain Gourbeyre enquired of Chief Corroller, the town's governor, if he had been granted any powers from the queen to negotiate. He was informed, equally formally, that none had been vouchsafed, and with salutes on both sides the envoy returned to the French ships, which were immediately ordered to begin bombarding the town.

The Merina army was famed for its bravery and the French no doubt expected a hard fight. Instead, minutes into the bombardment, a chance shot from one of the ships struck the ammunition store in the Merina fortifications. The magazine exploded with a deafening roar, and the French were gratified to see the defenders abandoning the fort and retreating into the forest. A force of 238 troops was immediately despatched from the ships and pursued the fleeing enemy for several miles, finally giving up the hunt at the Ivondrona river. Altogether, around 100 Merina fighters were killed in this brief clash of arms, while the French losses were put at nil. Twenty-three cannon and 200 muskets were found in the fortifications and taken as war booty. This utter routing of the mighty Merina soldiers, the ease with which it had been effected and the lack of casualties on the French side all made a marked impression on the local Betsimisaraka tribespeople who had witnessed the action. They immediately suggested an alliance with the foreign invaders; within a few days they promised to assemble between 6,000 and 8,000 armed men. Together, they and the French could march into the central highlands and annihilate the Merina once and for all.

There is little doubt that, had the French taken up the offer, they could well have reduced Merina power and brought Ranavalona to her knees. But time was not on Captain Gourbeyre's side: in a letter written on October 15, he states that the winter season was approaching – and the French knew from bitter experience the decimating effects of the tropical fevers that would surely follow if they took their forces inland. This,

•

and worries about leaving a vessel with a detachment of French soldiers in the harbour, caused Gourbeyre to decline the Betsimisaraka offer, and with it the chance of a quick victory against Ranavalona's forces. Instead, he contented himself with dislodging the Merina from their second main bastion on the east coast, at Foule Point.

Here, the French expedition attempted a repeat of the tactics that had proved so successful at Tamatave. And indeed, at first the action against Foule Point seemed to be a simple replaying of that earlier engagement. The French ships bombarded the Merina shore batteries and, while no magazine exploded, the enemy forces duly left their defences and fled into the nearby village. The French again made an amphibious landing and took their men confidently into the village, moving in extended formation and intending to clear it of any remaining enemy at the point of the bayonet. Here, quite unexpectedly, the victorious parallels with the Tamatave action were abruptly brought to an end.

As they reached the farthest side of the village, the French came upon a new fort, invisible from the shore – a fort full of defiant Merina soldiery and bristling with cannon and musket. Checked, but still confident, the attackers divided into two groups, one of which was to mount a direct attack on the Merina redoubt, while the second, composed of Yolof infantry under the command of a Captain Schoell, was delegated with the task of slipping around the side of the fortress to take the enemy in the rear. As the two columns began forming up, the seven or eight cannon in the Merina stronghold suddenly erupted in fire and smoke, shooting charge after charge of chain shot into the massed French troops. This had not been expected: the Merina were supposed to flee like sheep before the triumphant white men and their black auxiliaries. As the chain shot cut swathes through their ranks, the French panicked and fled *sauve qui peut* for the safety of the ships. Seeing the invaders in disarray, the Merina poured out from the fort in pursuit, and would undoubtedly have surrounded many of the fleeing Frenchman had it not been for the sangfroid of M Chareau, commanding the pinnace that was riding close to the shore. He covered the retreat with a fusillade of shells from his boat gun and gave the majority of his comrades the opportunity to reach the safety of the shoreline.

But not all of them: as he retreated, Captain Schoell received a bullet in his thigh and was unable to run as quickly as his companions. He was overtaken by the pursuing Merina, killed and swiftly beheaded. Six other Frenchmen were captured. All their heads were taken, and the grisly trophies impaled on poles placed along the shoreline by the victorious Merina as a warning to future invaders.

This one reverse had an incalculable effect on Merina morale. Although the French lost only 11 dead compared to the 75 losses sustained by the Merina, the fact remained that the invaders had been routed and forced to flee to their ships. The myth of French invincibility had been shattered, and this served not only to stiffen the resolve of the army, but also, when the welcome news (suitably embellished) reached Antananarivo, that of Queen Ranavalona and her advisers.

Why the French did not simply reform and press the attack on Foule Point remains a mystery. They had superior numbers and better armaments, and were well placed to quickly avenge their earlier defeat. Such an action would have done much to stem the rising tide of defiance among the Merina nobility. They chose, instead, to try their luck further along the coast at another Merina outpost, the former French stronghold of Larée Point. This time the French were far more respectful of Merina arms, bombarding the fort for a full two hours before deploying their landing force, which had since been reinforced by an additional 70 men. The fort was taken easily, with the loss of only one man, the defenders suffering 119 dead before abandoning their post and fleeing into the forest.

It appears that Captain Gourbeyre's plan was to reduce each of the Merina coastal strongpoints in turn, so leaving the defiant garrison at Foule Point isolated, and much more vulnerable to a final attack that would wipe out all Merina influence along the east coast. But each of their successes took time, and with the winter 'fever season' beginning the French were forced to pull back the bulk of their forces to the more salubrious climes of Reunion Island, leaving two vessels, *L'Infatigable* and *La Chevrette*, to defend the men stationed on their newly acquired Malagasy outposts.

Just before the French forces left, they received a delegation from Ranavalona carrying a conciliatory message offering commercial concessions to the invaders: French traders would be allowed to set up 'factories' along the coast wherever the Merina held sway. The offer was almost certainly authorised by Ranavalona as a panic response to the Merina defeat at Tamatave. The offer was a good one, and a considerable climb-down from the haughty obduracy to which Ranavalona had hitherto subjected all overtures from the invader. But no sooner had the offer been made than it was withdrawn, probably as a result of news of the French defeat at Foule Point reaching the capital. The French however, agonising over increasing British influence in the Merina capital, were certain that the machinations of English missionaries, serving the interests of 'perfidious Albion', were primarily to blame for the queen's intransigence.

From Reunion, the following year, the French despatched yet another mission of conciliation to the Sanguinary Queen. The mission was led by M Tourette, *secrétaire-greffier* of Ile Ste Marie, and M Rontaunay, a native of Reunion who owned a plantation on Madagascar and was well known to the Merina authorities. The two men split their forces and travelled by different routes, presumably in the hope of doubling their chances of reaching the notoriously hostile capital and its unsociable queen. Both failed: M Tourette was forbidden access to the capital and forced to kick his heels outside its walls for several weeks, until eventually giving up and making his way back down to the coast. Rontaunay was more successful: he made it through the gates of the city but was never granted audience with the queen. Ranavalona could see no reason for treating civilly what she considered a defeated enemy.

The French were not so easily put off, nevertheless. Madagascar continued to figure largely in rather grandiose plans for their 'inevitable' colonial expansion in the east. They still held bridge-heads on the Great Red Island at their recently acquired forts and, fired by an invincible confidence in their own martial prowess, they decided that what they could not obtain by negotiation they would take by force of arms. Even as its ambassadors were marking time in the long, humiliating and ultimately futile attempt to negotiate with Ranavalona, the French government was preparing to mount an even larger expedition against Madagascar, determined to remove this intransigent monarch from power by force or internal revolution. However, the gods of war seemed to hold Ranavalona as their darling. In the event, it was the French politicians who were swept away by an unlooked-for revolution in their own land.

When Louis XVIII of France had died intestate on September 16, 1824, the throne had passed to his younger brother, who ruled as Charles X. Four years earlier, King Louis had introduced an intricate, intrinsically unfair and deeply unpopular voting procedure designed to maximise the power of the wealthy. The newly crowned Charles soon proved himself to be an even more reactionary monarch. One of his first actions was to promulgate a law by which the nobility would be compensated for their losses at the time of the 1789 Revolution. The cost of the compensation was to be borne by the French upper middle classes, the very class whose support was vital to the king's political ambitions. The result of this ill-thought-out legislation was the complete alienation of this powerful group and a deep resentment that they were to nurture over the coming years.

When, even with his predecessor's blatantly skewed electoral system, Charles failed to obtain the compliant governing body he desired, he simply dissolved the legislature and tried again. The new elections were held on May 16, 1830 (just as the French efforts to subjugate Ranavalona were reaching their climax) and again Charles was disappointed in the outcome. This should, perhaps, have alerted the king to the feelings of deep dissatisfaction and anger simmering throughout France. But instead of moderating his policies, he pressed on with ever more repressive measures, formulating the so-called July Ordinances that aimed to establish total control of the press and effectively to rig all future elections by making it impossible to elect any but the most conservative and reactionary. It was a mistake of enormous proportions, and one that would cost him his throne. The great boil of resentment that had been festering and growing throughout the months finally burst. On July 28 the people of Paris rose in rebellion, and five days later Charles was forced to abdicate and to flee into exile.

The new revolutionaries, wary of the horrors that had proceeded from the policy of *liberté, égalité, fraternité* just 40 years earlier, eschewed a republic and turned instead to the popular Duke of Orleans, Louis-Philippe, offering him the crown. The duke's father had impeccable revolutionary credentials: he had renounced his privileges as Duke of Orleans and taken the name Philippe Egalité; he had voted for the execution of Louis XVI; and he had himself died under Madame Guillotine in November 1793. And now his son was crowned 'King of the French', a title chosen to demonstrate that the people themselves had chosen and accepted him as their ruler.

However, King Louis-Philippe proved a disappointment from the first. Unlike his father he had no interest in equality. Instead, he assiduously cultivated the upper middle class whose alienation had led to the downfall of Charles X. And while he was active in extending French power in Algeria, the proposed Madagascar adventure left him cold. The newly appointed ministers concurred, and the government gave out a statement that (for the present) France would abandon all its designs on Madagascar, 'while taking all necessary precautions to save the honour of our arms'. Despite the high-sounding phrases, 'rescue and retire' was the central French aspiration, and after another futile attempt at negotiating with *la reine sauvage* they evacuated Tintingue, their last stronghold on the mainland, on July 3, 1831. The retreat was watched by a 3,000-strong army of Merina troops, silent but triumphant – for the first time in many decades, Madagascar was free of French troops.

Ranavalona and her court were triumphant at this victory over the detested *vazah* (foreigners), and for a while the threat of invasion and oppression was lifted from the nation. But if things seemed to be returning to what passed for normal in Antananarivo and the rest of the country, it was a purely superficial normality. Ranavalona knew that, once again, all she had won for her country was a small breathing space – the French had not relinquished their colonial dreams. They would be back. And if they came, the British too would intensify their interest in Madagascar, intent on thwarting their rival's imperial designs. How could such formidable foes, armed with unlimited supplies of cannon and the most modern weaponry, be stopped indefinitely by her own army? Seen in the cold light of day, the victory over the French could only be viewed as an exceptional stroke of good fortune. None doubted the courage of the Merina warriors, but courage alone would not prevent the white man's victorious return.

The Merina had grown to be the most powerful tribe on Madagascar by trading slaves and produce for European muskets, powder and ball. But this advantage was, paradoxically, their greatest weakness, for they were entirely dependent on imported arms and only too vulnerable to a French or British blockade. If prosecuted with vigour, such an embargo would leave them weaponless and impotent, not only before the foreign invader but also before those other tribes they had so long harried and enslaved. Beyond the horizon and close at home, the storm clouds were gathering.

As the year of 1831 drew to a close, despite the protestations of the fetish priests that the national gods would continue to protect the kingdom, the future looked increasingly bleak. Ranavalona, pragmatist that she was, would not have been blind to the inexorable workings of realpolitik, and she can only have agonised over how long the Merina kingdom would continue to survive intact in the face of such a potent threat. In this darkest hour, fate brought Ranavalona the salvation of her nation in the most unlikely form of a shipwrecked French sailor.

# CHAPTER EIGHT

# The White Slave

**W**hen the waves of the Mozambique Channel cast Jean Laborde on the coarse sand of Madagascar's west coast, he could never have dreamed that within a year of his shipwreck he would be a man of fortune, respected and beloved of a queen. At this low point of his life, all his dreams of riches and renown seemed to have sunk with the loss of his ship.

The man who stood shivering and half naked on the Malagasy shore was a 26-year-old Gascon, whose lowly origin had not prevented him from embarking on a life of speculation and adventure. Jean Laborde had been born on October 16, 1805 in Auch, the son of a blacksmith and cartwright. He left school at twelve and, like most boys of his age and social class, he was expected to follow in his father's footsteps, which he did, serving his apprenticeship for five years. The time was not lost: it not only gave him an expertise in ironwork, but changed him from a gangly youth to a well-knit young man with massive chest and arms. However, Jean Laborde was not content. Some years earlier his father had produced harness and tackle for the horse of the future Marshal Lannes. Tales of military adventure, of battles and *la gloire* had sunk deeply into the impressionable psyche of the young Gascon. He knew that he could never be satisfied with the dull, quiet, predictable life of a village blacksmith. As soon as his apprenticeship was over, at the age of eighteen, Jean Laborde enlisted with the French army as a cavalryman. Adventure, fame and wealth beckoned.

But he was soon to be disillusioned. Distinction in war was the prime means of advancement for the miltary men of Laborde's day, and he longed to show his mettle on the field of valour. Unfortunately, the peaceful army of the Restoration left few avenues for aggressive encounters with a noble foe, and Laborde found his adventurous spirit stifled, his dreams confined to barracks, and his mind bored, restless and a prey to depression. Matters took so low a turn that he practised juggling and conjuring tricks in an attempt to pass the time, learning his techniques from travelling players who displayed their talents at the frequent local fairs. Strangely enough, this new-found and apparently worthless skill, born of frustration and despair, would save him from ruin and stand him in good stead during his later travels.

Laborde's army time passed slowly, but eventually he was free once again to choose his own destiny. He returned to his family home, but not to stay. He had long ago decided that he would not follow in his father's footsteps. To his own small savings his parents added a few modest ecus, and some weeks later Jean Laborde left home for a second attempt at fame and riches; he had tried the army, this time he would seek his fortune on the seas. He travelled west to the port city of Bordeaux, knowing only that he would board a ship for foreign parts. He had no preconceived plan and left his final destination to fate, deciding to take ship on whatever vessel was ready to sail when he arrived at the port. The first ship he found was bound for India. Destiny had chosen, and Laborde immediately paid for a one-way ticket to the subcontinent. The remainder of his meagre savings he spent on an assortment of glassware, scarves and other bric-a-brac. He believed now that he had found a sure way to repair his fortunes. He would become a street peddler, selling his wares among the bustling masses of Bombay.

The plan was wild, born of inexperience and the blind optimism of youth. But against all expectation, it worked wonderfully. Laborde used his expertise in prestidigitation, gleaned from his bored army days, to attract customers on the Bombay street corners. A large crowd would gather and, having won their goodwill and lulled them into a pleasant, affable mood with his juggling and conjuring tricks, he would then proceed to display his wares and to part as many of his audience as possible from their money. Within a short time Laborde had graduated to a street stall, which prospered greatly, and within a few years the penniless street trader from Gascony had become an affluent merchant, buying and selling a multitude of wares from a score of different countries. His path was set – a few more years' trading and he could return home a wealthy man.

And yet for Jean Laborde this success was not enough. He had left Auch, fleeing from the dull, predictable life of a tradesman, and he had sweated, planned and striven in Bombay to become ... a tradesman. The wheel had come full circle: destiny seemed intent on channelling his life into an unwanted and unwelcome path. He had, no doubt, achieved far more than he could have had he remained in his native Gascony. But what had become of his dreams of enterprise and hazard? Was he fated to dwell in hated routine, studying commodity prices and accounts all his life? His future seemed to stretch out before him like some vast, flat desert of limitless monotony.

By contrast, the sailors that he met during the course of his work seemed to live the sort of life he craved. Their tales excited and stirred his sense of adventure, leaving him feeling that the best years of his life were passing him by; passing profitably no doubt, but without that wonderful frisson of excitement that alone made life worth living. Sitting in the smoke-filled portside taverns, Laborde eagerly absorbed the fabulous tales of the rum-soaked sailormen he met there, stories of strange lands, lost ships and fabulous treasure. One Frenchman informed him of a huge store of gold on a lost island in the Mozambique Channel, just off the coast of Madagascar. Another spoke of a place in the strait where ten treasure ships lay sunk, their broken hulls stuffed full of rich cargo and barrels of gold; a third described the jewels and specie lying strewn around the shallow waters of the island of Juan de Novas. The treacherous reefs around Madagascar were the graveyard of many a fine galleon. And all a man needed, they affirmed, was a good ship and a stout heart and there was treasure aplenty along the Malagasy coast, the riches of Aladdin, the wealth of Solomon, all there for the taking.

These tales were more than Jean Laborde could bear. He was still a young man, just twenty-six years old, and naïve enough to believe in the truth of most of these tavern tales. He yearned for a swashbuckling life of risk and incident. After a few months of agonising indecision, he made up his mind. He would risk everything on a single throw. Quickly, he sold up his holdings in India and with the money chartered a boat and crew. The die was cast: he would seek out the lost ships, wrest their treasures from the bosom of the ocean, and return home with more gold than he could spend in seven lifetimes. But where to begin his quest? There was only one answer: Madagascar.

Again, his dreams of adventure led to disillusion and disappointment. For more than six months Laborde's hired schooner scouted up and down the Mozambique Channel, yet for all his searching, for all his expenditure, Laborde saw no profit. Stubbornly, he continued his quest into the worst season of the year, tempting fate and paying the price of his hubris. A huge storm, rushing up the Mozambique Channel, took Laborde's ship unawares and rent its sails, wave after enormous wave crashing down on the hapless vessel and pushing it closer and closer to the Malagasy shore. Rudderless, the tempest finally cast boat and crew against the sea rocks of Mahela where, under its incessant pounding, the ship began to break up. Through the mist and sea spray the doomed mariners could see the sandy beach of Madagascar's west coast just a few hundred yards away, tantalisingly out of reach in the tides and winds that even as they watched were tearing their ship, plank by plank and spar by spar, to pieces.

But if it was death to swim for the shore it was, equally, death to remain. Better, surely, to go down fighting against the odds than wait passively for the end? Never slow to risk his life on a single throw, Laborde plunged into the storm and struck out for the safety of the shore. How many others followed we do not know, but it seems that, apart from his negro servant, only he was fortunate enough to survive that short swim in such murderous waters. Morning found him desolate and exhausted on the sand of this mysterious island, more wretched and far poorer than when he had left France over five years before.

By chance, the waves had thrown Laborde on shore close to the lands of Napoleon de Lastelle, one of the few Creole planters on the Great Red Island, and one of the very few to be welcome at the court of Queen Ranavalona. De Lastelle fed and clothed the two men and lodged them at his own home. He took a liking to the unfortunate young Gascon whom fate had pitched up at his door, and allowed him to help around the plantation. De Lastelle was soon impressed by the intelligence and industry of his new guest and his many accomplishments. One talent in particular drew his eye – Laborde's skill with metals, a consequence of the long years he had spent as a youth at his father's forge in Auch. De Lastelle was deep in the queen's confidences and he knew of her desperate desire to diminish her kingdom's dependence on foreign arms. Ranavalona wanted to cast her own cannon, produce her own muskets, manufacture her own gunpowder. Only then could she escape the intolerable 'influence' that the European nations continued to exert over her realm.

Already she had tried to extract technological knowledge from the *vazah*, in the shape of another Frenchman shipwrecked earlier on her coast. By Merina law all castaways were the property of the crown, and this white slave of Ranavalona had been set up with his own workshop in Ilefy, some few miles from the capital, where he had been given the job of producing muskets. But the task had proved beyond his capacity and the project had been abandoned. In the shape of Jean Laborde, Napoleon de Lastelle believed that he had found the man to give the queen her desires. And in more ways than he can have imagined, he was right.

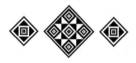

A few days later, Ranavalona was awakened from her siesta in the royal Rova by the arrival of Prince Coroller, a Bentaminene royal whose tribe had been conquered by King Radama many years before and who ever since had given loyal service to the Merina kingdom. A grandson of the English pirate Tom Tew, Prince Coroller's titles now included 'Victor of the Yolofs', since his successful action against the French auxiliaries, and 'Beautiful Eye', for the monocle of blue beryl that he held habitually in the socket of his blind eye. His distinctive lens was, perhaps, the only thing beautiful about him, for he was excessively ugly and riddled with syphilis, his face pockmarked and his teeth crumbling in rotting, mephitic gums. For all that he was a highly regarded member of the court, not only for his wise counsel, but because he alone knew the etiquette of the European courts and the language of the nation Ranavalona hated for its imperial pretensions but whose culture she aspired to – the French.

This grizzled warrior was received with the minimum of ceremony on the verandah of her private chambers. Before entering he removed his French low-heeled shoes and, honouring Merina tradition, stepped across the threshold with his right foot before advancing on the queen, his tricorn hat in his right hand, its plumes sweeping the floor. In his left hand he carried a package of the utmost importance, a letter from de Lastelle and addressed to the queen herself. True to her superstitious temperament, before she would accept the missive or even open it, she demanded that it be 'exorcised' of any baleful influences, purified three times, by holy water, by the ashes of the dead and by an incantation of the twenty-one magic syllables. This done, Prince Coroller began the translation.

Ranavalona listened to his words with increasing attention and excitement: a Frenchman, a Gascon of twenty-six years, cast up on her coast and 'as a victim of shipwreck, he is, it goes without saying, your slave'. But what a Frenchman! 'Strong, enterprising, intelligent, skilled in engineering and mechanics', he had already begun learning the Malagasy language and had adapted himself to the customs of the country. Then suddenly, she was sitting forward on her divan, her eyes alight with excitement as Prince Coroller continued the translation in deep, measured tones:

> Jean Laborde is exactly the man you require. He knows how to cast cannon, to bore musket barrels and to manufacture powder.

At last! Ranavalona leapt to her feet and danced across the room, unable to contain herself, royal dignity forgotten. Her prayers had finally been answered.

Shaking with excitement, she ordered the prince to send her fleetest porters and lightest sedan chair to bring her new white slave to the capital. She impressed upon Coroller the importance of his mission: it was imperative that the Frenchman be brought up to Antananarivo as soon as possible. The fate of the nation depended on his skills. Then, with her slave girls and favourites, she gave herself up to rejoicing.

It took twelve days for even the most light-footed porters to cover the 100 leagues between De Lastelle's plantation and the high plateau, for the way was difficult, past swamps and lagoons and along narrow paths through steep passes. Nor was it possible for strangers to travel straight to the capital. Antananarivo was a sacred place, and it was forbidden, under pain of death, for any wayfarer, and especially the *vazah*, to approach without permission. By tradition, every caravan, every traveller, must stop at Ambatoumanga, some four leagues distant, and await the queen's pleasure. The wait was a form of quarantine, giving the monarch's officials the chance to examine the traveller's motives and belongings, and for the priests to examine the portents, the sacrifices and the *sikidy*, to foretell the consequences for the queen and the nation of the newcomer's arrival and, if favourable, to determine an auspicious date for his entry into the city.

After his almost two-week journey through the wilderness, with nothing more to break the monotony than the occasional impoverished village, Jean Laborde's first sight of Antananarivo can only have seemed like a dream. Perched atop the steep escarpment of red rock and clinging to the surrounding slopes, the Village of a Thousand Villages shimmered proudly in the clear mountain air. And above all, dominating the capital, sharply outlined against the highest peaks and the azure of the sky, was the place his fate would be decided – the steep-roofed Rova of Antananarivo, the royal enclosure of Ranavalona-Manjaka, the by-now infamous Sanguinary Queen of Madagascar.

He need not have feared. Indications that his presence was welcome arrived in the form of gifts from the Great Glory herself – boxes of fowl, beef fat, panniers of eggs, fruit, jars of honey, all were laid in his path. The omens were apparently so favourable that tradition was set aside and Laborde's caravan was given special dispensation to complete the final stage of its journey to the capital several days ahead of schedule. He was carried there in some style, followed by his negro servant, who wore a green turban and bore himself so nobly that the Malagasy watchers immediately named him Ramenti, 'Mr Black'. Behind the white slave and his black footman came a long line of porters, bearing, as tradition demanded, presents for the queen from de Lastelle. As they approached the entrance to the city, Ranavalona ordered a salute of muskets to be fired. It was, perhaps, a form of sympathetic magic, for Laborde, the putative arms maker, entered the capital wreathed in the smoke of musketry and the smell of gunpowder.

Antananarivo's inhabitants watched the advent of the queen's white slave with undisguised interest: word of his skill in producing firearms was already common knowledge in the city. Generally, all *vazah* were treated with the utmost suspicion; the Malagasy believed that most were cannibals and would happily feast on them if given the chance. But this *vazah* was different: in an old Malagasy legend a shipwrecked white man marries the daughter of a king and later rules the kingdom, dispensing justice and plenty. This alone, without his weapon-making talents, was sufficient to mark Jean Laborde out as special. But there was more. A second story was circulating in Antananarivo: that an old man of the city had dreamed a strange dream, where white bulls had bounded from the foaming waves and coupled with the willing heifers of Madagascar. A song went round:

> *He! He! Our pretty queen.*
> *He! He! The white bull.*

Skill in metalworking and military hardware aside, there was little doubt that the Malagasy people had a very clear idea of what the queen would demand of her new white slave.

# CHAPTER NINE

# The Queen's Bath

The success against the French and her good fortune in finding Laborde made Ranavalona's position as absolute ruler of the Merina unassailable. Only one beloved of the gods could have vanquished the hated *vazah* and driven them into the sea, and at the same time been sent a slave whose knowledge made the enemy's threatened return far more unlikely. Under her rule the Merina were once again undisputed rulers of the Great Red Island, and her possession of Jean Laborde and his gun-making abilities made the continuance of Merina hegemony surer still. All Imerina believed that the hour had come to demonstrate their nation's puissance in time-honoured fashion, by punitive expeditions against the conquered tribes. These raids were a recurrent feature of Malagasy life and served two main purposes: they acted as a deterrent, 'persuading' the tributary states how ill judged and impolitic it would be to rebel against Merina rule (an important consideration should the Europeans return); and the booty and slaves obtained by these onslaughts were an important source of wealth and income, keeping both army and nobles satisfied.

Just after the evacuation of the French stronghold at Tintingue, Ranavalona launched two punitive expeditions from

Antananarivo. The first, sent to the west under the command of one Ravalontsalama, made a successful, if sanguinary, progress through the tributary states. While passing through one Sakalava district, the army became suspicious that the people were hiding arms in preparation for insurrection. They put many men to the *tanguena* ordeal, which most failed. These poor unfortunates were bound and cast into a ditch outside the village, where they remained for two days without food or drink and guarded at all times. At the end of this time they were dragged out and crucified on posts 'at short distances from one another, forming a long line of excruciating agony round their village'. The remainder of the inhabitants, numbering over 2,000 people, were sent to Antananarivo to be sold as slaves.

A second, larger force was sent to the south. It was under the command of Rainiharo (who with his brothers had contrived the death of Ranavalona's former lover Andrianmihaja and taken his place in her bed). This army was protected by the national idol Rakelimalaza, which was carried with the troops to strengthen their morale. There appears to have been no strategic plan, no firm objective to this mission, except to terrorise the populace and seize booty. As the troops moved through the land of the Betsileo they came upon a friendly village of about 300 families and set up camp close by. The Merina officers, in a gesture of goodwill, invited the headman and all the men of the village to a banquet at the camp, an invitation that the village folk happily accepted. Then, as they waited for their meal:

> the drums beat out a signal, upon which the soldiers seized their victims and, leading them outside the camp, deliberately put them to death with spears. The women and children were all taken as plunder. The second officer in command on this occasion, Ramahafadrahona, boasted that he had killed eleven of them with his own hands.

One of the intended victims managed to escape and he took word of the Merina's treachery to Ikongo, the next village on the army's line of march. This settlement possessed an excellent defensive position, strongly walled and situated atop a steep rock, accessible only by a narrow and precipitous path. After their easy massacre, Rainiharo's army found Ikongo a much tougher nut to crack – bristling with armed men and ready for a fight.

The Merina force set up their artillery on a level plain close to the village and laid down fire on the walls, under cover of which the infantry moved forward up the narrow footway to the assault. Flushed with their earlier success and confident of victory by virtue of the presence of the god Rakelimalaza, hundreds of camp followers accompanied the soldiers, crowding their way up the restricted path, intent on getting their share of the plunder when the village was taken. But the men of Ikongo, aroused by the earlier massacre and knowing they faced certain death if the town was taken, put up such a spirited resistance that they succeeded in forcing the Merina soldiery back from the walls. Expecting an easy victory but seeing their army retire in confusion, the camp followers panicked and fled in disorder, taking with them many of the Merina army. However, the narrow path could not contain such an outflow of people and in the horror and hysteria of the moment over 2,000 of the attackers were toppled headlong over the edge of the cliff to their deaths, among them the boastful and treacherous Ramahafadrahona.

This stain on Merina arms could not be allowed to pass unanswered, and early the next year an even larger army, of around 10,000 men, marched out of Antananarivo, carrying rape and murder to the lands of the south. Under the command of Rainiharo they cut a path of terror through the country, seizing grain, driving off cattle, killing men and carrying away the women and children into slavery.

Where force of arms would not suffice Rainiharo did not scruple to use guile and deceit. At the town of Ivato they found that the inhabitants' numbers had been swelled by reinforcements from the surrounding lands, with around ten or twelve chieftains and their men spoiling for a fight. The town itself occupied an almost impregnable position on a high hill, surrounded on all sides by steep slopes. Realising that a frontal assault was doomed to failure, Rainiharo sent heralds forward to proclaim that, if the inhabitants would but lay down their arms, no harm would come to them.

On the first day this announcement was scorned by the men of Ivato, but Rainiharo persisted, sending the heralds out several times each day with his offer of peace. By the third day divisions had arisen within the town: around half of the defenders were adamant that they would never surrender, while the rest counselled conciliation with so powerful a foe and were willing to place their trust in the Merina promise of safe conduct. Eventually, it was agreed that all those who wished to continue the struggle should escape during the night through the dense forest that adjoined one side of the town, and that the following day the settlement would be handed over to Rainiharo and his men. When dawn broke around 20,000 inhabitants remained within Ivato's walls, and these:

> *being again assured of the most friendly dispositions towards them, delivered up their muskets, spears, etc. They were surrounded by soldiers, and all the men found capable of carrying a spear were ordered to pass from one circle of soldiers to another, whilst the women and children remained within the first circle. They were carefully examined as they passed along to see whether they had yet concealed any weapons about them. The soldiers then commenced tying their hands with cords. They now saw the fatal treachery, and those who were not bound made desperate efforts to rush through the ranks; but few got out, and those that were bound were killed at leisure the following day. The carnage commenced early in the morning and lasted until late in the afternoon. The army then returned, flushed with their success, to the capital, bringing ten thousand captives.*

The influx of slaves and booty stimulated the Imerina economy and increased the optimism that Jean Laborde's arrival had engendered in the population. Ranavalona had already put her white slave to work, and in more ways than one. De Lastelle had informed the queen that the young Frenchman's knowledge extended to ironwork and she was eager to see if her new acquisition could indeed produce the weapons she so desperately needed to hold her realm secure. But rumour was rife that the queen depended on the Gascon adventurer for far more than economic development and national security – according to the gossipmongers of Antananarivo, the 'white bull dream' had already come to pass.

This is almost certainly the case. Though the accounts of the time are extremely discreet on the issue, it was readily acknowledged that the queen's sexual appetite was enormous. As the bearer of the divine *sang real*, she carried a blood so elevated in Malagasy eyes that it could not be further ennobled by any union, however advantageous. Nor, conversely, could it be degraded by the blood of the meanest slave. The queen could couple with whomever she might wish, and by all accounts this is exactly what she did do, and on a prodigious scale, having as permanent lovers the two brothers Rainiharo and Rainimaharo and at the same time holding her 'bodyguard' of eight 'sparrow-hawks' as a masculine ruler might keep a harem. Laborde was around thirty years old when he was brought to the Imerina capital, tall, well-knit, handsome with an 'imperial' goatee (though apparently with receding hair and a pronounced 'widow's peak'). He was, as the French say, a *bel homme*, a type to which Ranavalona was especially partial (her eight sparrowhawks were composed of just such men).

We need not imagine that this liaison was the love of either Ranavalona's or Jean Laborde's life: the queen used men for a space and then discarded them, and there is no reason to suppose that she treated her white slave any differently. But she was not unkind to those who pleased her, and she knew how to reward loyalty. And if the stories are correct, it was Jean Laborde who achieved the seemingly impossible and gave the queen, at the relatively advanced age of forty-one, a child, and a son to boot. If true, the partiality she showed to the shipwrecked Gascon over the space of several decades would be all the easier to explain.

Whatever the truth, it does seem that following the young Frenchman's arrival, the queen entered much more into a spirit of enjoyment of the various Malagasy festivals. Chief among these revels was the Fanandrano, a huge annual celebration that combined religious, civic and nationalistic functions with a wild, five-day bacchanalia that culminated in a part-religious, part-voluptuous rite unique to Madagascar culture: the Queen's Bath.

Much effort went into the staging of the Fanandrano. For a month prior to the feast the roads to Antananarivo were thronged with herds of wild bulls, with porters carrying panniers of food and drink, and staggering under enormous loads of aromatic timber that would be needed to feed the many sacrificial fires that the ceremony demanded. At the same time, royal heralds were sent into all parts of the Merina territories to call the people to the capital, to eat *jaka* with Ranavalona-Manjaka and to receive the blessings of her solemn Bath. All responded (for it was death to refuse the queen) and an endless, colourful cavalcade of people, palanquins and horsemen converged on the capital from all directions. In contrast to most other occasions, where the various castes of nobles vied to outdo each other with the latest and most outlandish European and Arabic fashions, only traditional garments were apparent in the crowds. The Fanandrano was, among many other things, a celebration of the nation's history and culture, a veneration of the times and beliefs of the ancestral shades. For this one period Imerina returned to its ancient ways, to a time before the coming of the *vazah*.

The holiday began with a Malagasy version of the Pamplona bull run, when the queen ordered the release of an enormous herd of wild bulls, which hurtled down the steep, narrow streets of the city, scattering the assembled revellers. The bulls belonged to whomever could catch and control them, but only on condition that their new owners brought the beasts to the forum of Andouale, where the sacred stone of the Merina coronation ceremony stood in its solitary glory. Here, in the presence of more than 100,000 spectators, the bulls were tormented by revellers who screamed at them, threw stones, shook red cloths and hung onto their horns until, goaded to a frenzy of excitement and terror, the poor beasts struck out, charging their tormentors, throwing men, women and children into the air and trampling them underfoot. In response, hundreds of javelins were cast, the frenzied spectators screaming 'To the death! To the death!' as the spears struck home. A second release of bulls completed the frenzied melee:

> men and wild bulls rolling in the sticky mud, among the burst entrails, and the place of the Sacred Stone was no more than an immense barbaric arena where the Madagascans relive their ancestral hours of magnificent cruelty.

As the sun set on the first day, aromatic torches and bonfires were lit and turned the city into a perfumed sparkling jewel set amid the twelve sacred mountains. The fires burned throughout the night, and dawn brought more sanguinary entertainment in the form of almost endless bullfights. These were not the combats favoured by the Spanish, but deadly contests that pitted bull against bull, a fencing of sharpened horns that did not cease until one or other of the contestants was dead. The sport was very popular and most nobles kept a stable of fighting bulls, on which they lavished enormous care and attention. While European gentry were still in the habit of settling a matter of honour at dawn with pistols or sabres, the Malagasy aristocracy had devised a much more humane method of reconciling their differences. They brought their bulls to the field of honour and let them fight a proxy battle to decide the issue.

Ranavalona was a true aficionado of these battles, betting heavily on the contests, following her favourite bulls and anxiously awaiting the outcome. The death of a bull apparently affected her deeply. It was said that, while she could condemn hundreds to the most excruciating deaths without the slightest intimation of remorse, the loss of one of her stable of bovine fighters would send her into paroxysms of grief and rage. When her most favourite bull was gored to death:

> she wept much and bitterly, and it was long before she would take comfort. The animal was buried with all the honours accorded to a grandee of the State. It was wrapped in a number of simbus and covered with a great white cloth and the marshals had to lay it in the grave ... Two great stones are placed upon the grave, in memory of the dear departed; and the queen is said to think of him still with gentle sorrow.

Such a gladiatorial disaster was, however, a very rare event, for the simple reason that the queen's bulls seldom lost a fight. Such an enviable record was due, it was said, to a powerful talisman that had been bequeathed to her by the late King Radama, a magic amulet that guaranteed victory. This may well have been the case, but given the spleen such defeats incited in the queen and the fatal danger of displeasing the Great Glory, it is likely that most nobles facing Ranavalona's bulls took great care to ensure that their own bull went down to ignominious defeat.

The third day brought the most important rite of the whole festival, the Queen's Bath. In sharp contrast to the *son et lumière* of the previous evening, as night fell over the city all the people were required by law to extinguish their torches and bonfires. On the eve of the Queen's Bath – and for that one sacred night alone – only a single light was visible in the whole of the darkened capital. Shining in from the brooding mass of the palace perched above the town, the flame of the Queen-Goddess Ranavalona-Manjaka burned in glorious solitude.

The ceremony took place the following afternoon in the main hall of the Silver Palace, its walls and floors decorated with wonderful frescos and skilful marquetry contrived by Legros and the British soldiers that King Radama had brought to the capital. Half concealed behind purple curtains, an ancient *cuveau* was visible, filled with water. The air in the room was stifling, for the rest of the premises were brimful of the great and the good of Imerina society. The nobility of Antananarivo crushed together with invited guests from all the different regions of the kingdom, all dressed alike in the *simbu*, the Malagasy toga, strewn with gems and in their best finery. The men and women were kept separate, but all were scarcely able to breathe in the cramped, confined space of the lavishly adorned chamber. Outside, a vast multitude of the hoi polloi waited impatiently, hooting, spitting and pushing restlessly against the restraining spear hafts of the palace guards.

Suddenly, massed rifles barked from the courtyard, and to the sound of seven volleys of musket fire Ranavalona made her appearance. Her head and her feet were uncovered, she was draped in a long purple cloak, and it was obvious to all that beneath this covering the queen was naked. Accounts differ as to what happened next. Some say that the monarch was transported to her throne on the crossed arms of her two main ministers/lovers, the brothers Rainiharo and Rainimaharo. From there, having received the adulation of the crowds, she was carried, accompanied by her ladies-in-waiting, behind a screen where the bath had been made ready. Others recount that the ceremony began with the Tsitialainga, the silver spear borne forward and presented to the populace. The queen then appeared, walking beneath a purple canopy of silk, carried on slender poles of ivory by four hand-maidens and followed by four more females holding a three-sided screen, open at one side. Once again, the assembled multitude burst into applause, crying *Manjaka! Manjaka!* (Majesty! Majesty!) and holding out their hands to the queen-goddess. As they did so, the maids carrying the screen moved around the object of adulation and, veiled in mystery, Ranavalona entered the bath.

Now, all that could be heard was the sound of water being laved over the invisible figure of the queen, the sound continuing for several minutes until the screen was suddenly removed and Ranavalona stood once more before the crowd in her cloak, her face flushed, her long black tresses hanging wetly against the red silk. She carried in her hand a large white horn, the *tandrompotsy*, intricately chased with precious metal. The horn was filled with water from the queen's bath, and Ranavalona now walked forward and proceeded to sprinkle its contents over the assembled multitude. As the (to modern minds) dirty bath-water struck individuals in the crowd, they gave voice to great gasps of delight. For the Merina, such a dowsing was conceived as a great honour, for the water from the bath was believed to be imbued with all the magical virtue embodied in the queen's person, with spiritual power and fecundity. As Ranavalona had been purified in the sacred bath, so they too were purified by even the smallest contact with her bath-water. Like the Christian baptism, it was a new beginning.

Her duties completed, the queen withdrew to thunderous applause and the guests began to leave. But the crowd outside, no longer constrained by the queen's soldiery, could at last press forward and fall upon the now-empty bath, fighting each other for the opportunity to bathe their limbs in the sacred water. The bath was drained and filled again, the water from the second rinsing being carried away as a charm against all ills. Drained and filled a third time, the water was sprinkled over Imerina's paddy fields to increase their fertility and ensure an abundant harvest.

Given the power and devotion the ceremony engendered, it is incredible to discover that it was entirely an invention of Ranavalona's shrewd and calculating mind. It seems that she conceived this rite herself, as, apart from an ambiguous reference to a bath taken by her husband, King Radama, there does not appear to be any mention of the ceremony in the oral tradition of Imerina. Nor is it recorded later in the *Tantaran'ny Andriana*, the 'History of the Nobility' collated by the Roman Catholic missionary Father Callet during his stay in Antananarivo between 1864 and 1865. If Ranavalona did invent the Queen's Bath, the ceremony bears witness to her instinctive understanding of theatre and to her almost preternatural understanding of mass psychology. The whole ceremony was beautifully choreographed and loaded with symbolic meaning. From start to finish, the rite was designed as a means of elevating Ranavalona's status, to separate her even from the highest rank of nobles, to deify her and, perhaps even more important, to make evident to the ordinary people her status as a goddess.

But she was an accessible goddess. Immediately following the ceremony of the Queen's Bath, a species of communion, a eucharist, took place, a ritual meal in which all felt themselves to be blessed merely by participating. Huge cauldrons of boiling water, fed by bonfires, were established in the palace and on the surrounding courtyards, in which enormous quantities of Madagascar's staple food – rice – were set to cook, carefully watched over by the royal slaves. While the enormous stewpots bubbled steadily, a multitude of long, brown strips of preserved beef (sun dried and capable of remaining edible for years, even in Madagascar's tropical heat) was made ready. This was *jaka*, what the French called *boucan* and the food that gave the name *boucannier* or buccaneer to numerous generations of pirates.

When everything was prepared, cannons were fired to the four points of the compass, their thunder echoing back from the surrounding hills, to alert the divine ancestors that the feast was about to begin. For this ritual was also a banquet of the dead, and the national manes were believed to gather on the Hill of Bulls near the capital each year, in expectation of their time-honoured feast. As the ancestral ghosts sped their way towards the palace, the meal began with the Maréchal maitre-queux (head chef), preceded by the two first ministers, carrying a plate of solid gold to the queen, on which was placed a portion of rice and a single piece of *jaka*. The two first ministers, Renihar and Renijohary, preceded the offering and knelt next to the throne. As the golden dish was laid before her, Ranavalona, in her role now as a Malagasy *pontifex maximus*, as high priestess of the Merina, used her sceptre to bless the meat and, in the sonorous tones of ecclesiasts everywhere, called out that today the people ate this meal in communion with the sacred dead, so that they would preserve them from evil and bestow their blessings upon the nation.

Then, taking up a portion of rice on a small dagger, she pressed the grains hard against the forehead of the kneeling Rainiharo, declaring in a loud voice that it was not the rice that was holy, it was Rainiharo, that he was holy because of her own purification and her blessing, that he was holy by virtue of celebrating this feast and remembering the ancestors and their customs. Renihojary took Rainiharo's place and the ritual and the wording were repeated. Then, rising from her throne, Ranavalona began a chant of *Bonheur! Bonheur!* (Blessings! Blessings!), all the while scattering the remaining rice broadcast over the assembled people, each of whom cried out with joy whenever a grain from the sacred meal touched his head. Further off, the majority of the onlookers, those with no chance of receiving a direct blessing, began their meals of *jaka* and rice. The meal was served by slaves, in the ancient manner, on banana leaves; and to please the shades present at the feast, people ate the frugal repast with their fingers, in the manner of their forefathers.

The next morning, the time of spartan self-denial was brought to an end. If the previous day had been devoted to death and communion with the ancestral shades, this dawn brought a celebration of life and the many joys of living. As queen, Ranavalona was the possessor of huge numbers of zebu cattle, and she used them now to bestow her largesse on the whole of the Merina nation. Ten thousand fat cattle were offered to the army and the people, and more to the allies and the few English missionaries who remained at the capital. Antananarivo resounded to the sound of slaughter, the pavings of the steep streets ran with blood, and the sweet smell of roasting beef ascended in wreaths into the clear blue sky above the Village of a Thousand Villages.

As night fell the rigid hierarchy of the eleven castes was thrown aside and the populace, gorged on blood and flesh, broke free of all traditional restraints. Like the ancient Roman Saturnalia and similar ceremonies of many other societies, the normal rules of behaviour were turned on their head: for this one night the slaves were emancipated and conversed with their masters as equals, the streets were thronged with torch-carrying naked and semi-naked revellers, drinking and feasting and accosting with licentious intent whomever took their fancy. Panmixia was the order of the day. Total strangers coupled in public, urged on by the drunken crowd, servant with noble, freeman with slave, for none was permitted to refuse another on this night of licence when, between a single sunset and dawn, the traditional restraints of custom and morality were suspended. The Malagasy believed that this unbridled outpouring of sexual energy affected far more than the couples involved: copulation at this time fecundated the whole world, improving the fertility of livestock and the yield from the fields.

Nor was the palace exempt from this rite of carnal excess. The queen enjoined all her courtiers to comply with these customs and was foremost in prosecuting the tradition with the utmost rigour. One account, possibly apocryphal, gives an indication of how seriously she took the bacchanalia. According to this report, the queen's new favourite, Sirima, refused to take part in the palace revels, rejecting the advances of a 'sparrowhawk' who had already enjoyed the favours of the queen. This young woman was a pupil of Mrs Griffiths, the wife of one of the English residents, and had taken to heart the Christian admonition to eschew all such heathen orgies. Ranavalona was outraged by her favourite's attitude, though whether she fumed because Sirima had dared to refuse a lover she herself had just accepted or was simply infuriated that foreign ethics had managed to breach this celebration of Merina tradition, it is not possible to determine.

Whatever the reason, in the face of the young woman's stubborn refusal to participate in the darker aspects of this night of misrule, Ranavalona demonstrated her displeasure and the total power she possessed over her subjects. She called to her side her executioner, a negro of enormous stature, a consummate sadist skilled in the horrendous arts of the *tsimandao*, and ordered him to take the still-recalcitrant Sirima and to rape her before the eyes of the laughing, bacchic assembly of nobles and slaves. As the act took place, the queen is said to have called out jeeringly that, although Sirima could read and write, she seemed to have forgotten the most important of all feminine accomplishments – how to receive a man with style and skill.

The Fanandrano harked back to a Merina golden age, grounding the nation in a heroic time of simplicity, before the arrival of the European powers with their outlandish costumes, printing presses, machines and superior weapons. It was retreat into myth, symptomatic of the nation's desire to escape the problems of the present. But the festival's traditional pleasures could not forever distract Ranavalona and her ministers from the political realities of 1833. Word was brought to Antananarivo that the French had revived their project to invade and colonise Madagascar, and the queen's white slave, Jean Laborde, was set to work to provide the necessities for repelling any potential incursion.

Laborde rose to the challenge magnificently. He had soon discovered that the workshops at Ilafy, given to him for the production of muskets, cannon and powder, were wholly inadequate to the task. He therefore prevailed on the queen to transfer materiel and workers from Ilafy to a new site that he had chosen at Mantasoa, about 40 kilometres outside the capital. The area was ideal for his purposes and possessed a profusion of natural resources. It was supplied with an abundance of wood and iron ore; and it had a multitude of streams that could be used to power the great number of machines that Laborde was already planning.

It may be that by this time Ranavalona and Laborde were lovers and she would refuse her new favourite nothing. But whatever the reason, the Gascon adventurer received full support from the queen, and was given carte blanche to pursue his plans. The area became a hive of activity. In just a few years, under the watchful and ever-present eyes of Jean Laborde, Mantasoa became a huge industrial complex. Built largely by corvée labour at tremendous human cost, huge aqueducts channelled water to the workshops, and row upon row of furnaces sprang up, producing iron, copper and steel to supply the numerous work- shops that lay scattered around the plateau. These manufactured an enormous range of materials: sulphuric acid, potassium, paints, soaps, glass, pottery, porcelain, bricks, tiles, cement, lime, dyes, rum, everything that a civilised nation could want or need.

Thanks to Laborde's drive, ingenuity and enterprise, Madagascar had become all but self-sufficient, with no need for foreign goods. This shipwrecked Frenchman had, single- handedly, brought the Industrial Revolution and its manifold benefits to Africa and made it thrive. But central to the whole complex, and the origin of this enterprise, was another less benign European development – the arsenal – where Laborde manufactured those objects dearest to his queen's heart. Muskets and cannon, shells and grenades rolled from the factories, destined for her army, and all of a quality to match any European arms. Now at last her soldiers could face the hated *vazah* on equal terms!

Over and above all his other duties, amorous and industrial, in 1834 the remarkable Frenchman was able to achieve an architectural triumph that excited the admiration of the world.

Using only native materials, he constructed for the queen an enormous ornate wooden palace, which at the time and for many years thereafter was the largest timber building in the world. Set atop the highest crag of Antananarivo, the building dominated the skyline for miles around, a fitting symbol of Ranavalona's ascendancy. The queen was rightly proud of her new abode, which was described by one traveller as:

> consisting of a ground floor and two stories, surmounted by a peculiarly high roof. The stories are surrounded by broad galleries. Around the building are pillars also of wood, eighty feet high, supporting the roof, which rises to a height of forty feet above them, resting in the centre on a pillar no less than one hundred and twenty feet high. All these columns, the one in the centre not excepted, consist of a single trunk; and when it is considered that the woods which contain trees of sufficient size to furnish these columns are fifty or sixty English miles from the capital, that the roads are nowhere paved, and in some places quite impassable, and that all the pillars are dragged hither without the help of a single beast of burden, or any kind of machine, and are afterwards prepared and set up by means of the simplest tools, the building of this palace may with truth be called a giant undertaking, and the palace itself be ranked among the wonders of the world. In bringing home the chief pillar alone, five thousand persons were employed, and twelve days were occupied in its erection.

# CHAPTER TEN

# The Coming Storm

In late 1834 two incidents occurred that were to have far-reaching consequences for every Christian on the island. A noble of high standing presented himself at the palace and asked for an audience with the queen. This was granted, and he entered the throne room of the great wooden palace, to find Ranavalona seated in majesty. She immediately required of him the reason for the meeting, and was told, 'I have come to ask your majesty for a spear, a bright sharp spear; grant my request.'

A great silence descended on the cool, shady room – the petition was incomprehensible, bizarre. Finally, Ranavalona broke the silence, demanding to know the reason for such a strange appeal. Without hesitation, the chief answered that he had watched in dismay as the influence of the foreign missionaries had dishonoured the Merina's traditional gods and the memory of the royal ancestors:

> whereby the nation is being deprived of their protection, to which alone it owes its safety. The hearts of the people are already turned from the customs of their ancestors, and from Her Majesty, their successor. By their instructions, their brotherhood

*and their books, the foreigners have already secured to their interests many men of rank and wealth in the army and offices of the government, many among the farmers and peasantry, and vast numbers of the slaves.*

He added that the foreigners were subverting the state and when the time was ripe they would send word for their army to appear and take possession of the kingdom, an easy task seeing that by that time the whole of the nation would be alienated from the government and the throne. He ceased speaking and there was complete silence in the throne room. He continued boldly:

*Such will be the issue of the foreign teaching and I do not wish to see that calamity come upon our country; to see our own slaves employed against us. Therefore I ask for a spear, to pierce my heart. That I may die before that evil day comes.*

The queen was said to have been much shaken by the request. Up until this time she had mainly tolerated the work of the missionaries, especially those protestant evangelists from the London Missionary Society, and their influence had grown over the passing years. But her chieftain's request had thrown the crucial question with regard to the foreigners into sharp focus: was she prepared to see the *vazah*'s culture and religion begin to dominate the land of Imerina? Did she, the symbol and guardian of her nation, wish to watch over an irreversible alteration of the country's established customs and usages?

Even after this event, it is not certain that Ranavalona would have chosen the course she did, had a strange new 'Christian' prophet not arisen in the land. His name was Rainitsiandavaka, and he had formerly been the guardian of an Imerina fetish named Izanaharitsimandry, 'the god who does not rest'. Rainitsi was prone to fits of depression and during one of these he chanced upon one of the jewels in the crown of the London Missionary Society, an eminent convert named Raintsiheva. The latter exhorted him to be of good cheer, and expounded to him the Good News of the Christian Bible. The teachings appeared to work, for the fetish guardian soon recovered his former good spirits, and immediately transferred his spiritual allegiance to the god of the Europeans.

Unfortunately, either the instruction given by the foreign missionaries to Raintsiheva had itself been deficient, or in his melancholia Rainitsi did not listen too clearly to the details, and the meeting had the most disastrous consequences. Rainitsi did not simply convert to Christianity; instead, he took elements from his original fetish beliefs and melded them with Christian concepts of the origin of humanity, universal peace, resurrection of the dead and so on, to produce a syncretistic religion of his own. Not content with this, Rainitsi began preaching this religion to his fellow Malagasy, many of whom were so taken with its precepts they gave up their former beliefs and became his disciples. As the sect grew larger its leader was seized with the grandiose idea of converting the whole of Madagascar to his novel theological doctrine, and set off with many of his followers to the capital, where he proposed to speak with the queen and effect her conversion to the new faith.

Ranavalona's spies and agents had kept her well informed of the sect's activities. To her, Rainitsi's new quasi-Christian religion was just another thorn in her side, one more problem derived from the foreigners that might result, like the work of the foreign Christians, in disintegration of the delicate social balance on which her rule rested. And while she hesitated to act against the missionaries, she had no such scruples with home-grown threats to her authority. Before they had even reached Antananarivo, she had ordered Rainitsi and his followers arrested. The self-styled prophet, and three of his principal lieutenants, were summarily executed, and 70 (in all likelihood a distorted reflection of the '70' of the New Testament) were put to the *tanguena* ordeal, from which a further 18 died.

The new religion was crushed utterly, but the affair had almost as severe a repercussion on the future of orthodox Christianity in the island. Rainitsi had been greatly influenced by the teachings of the foreign religion and, in the mind of the queen and her followers, this connection could only undermine the standing of the Christian converts and their teachers. From now on they were both viewed with even graver suspicion than before.

In the course of crushing Rainitsi's new religion, all his remaining followers were sold into slavery, and this action had a further disastrous effect on the future security of Madagascar's Christian community. The queen and her officers gained much profit from the sale, and they were not slow to realise that oppressing the followers of the foreign religion would not only protect Malagasy religion and culture, it would have the added benefit of swelling the coffers of the persecutors. Rainitsi's followers had been numbered in hundreds – the missionaries counted their converts in thousands.

But before such a plan could be put into effect, external events changed everything. On August 23, 1834, the British government had promulgated the Emancipation Act, freeing all slaves within the British empire. It was a triumph for the abolitionists, but it came just too late for their champion, William Wilberforce, who had died aged 73 less than a month before the Act became law. The legislation was not merely humane: recognising the significant shift in economics that abolition would entail, it included provision for a gradual, step-wise emancipation of all slaves and for compensating slave owners. These far-sighted provisions effectively defused the most vocal opposition, a lesson that the United States failed to understand with disastrous results just twenty-seven years later.

But for all its insight in placating the slave owners by passing the Emancipation Act, Britain effectively declared war on the slave trade worldwide, or at least wherever British naval power could enforce its prohibition, which included Madagascar. Thanks to the annual depredations of her army, Ranavalona's government had provided slaves to the West Indies and American trade, to the European Indian Ocean colonies, and to the Arab and Bombay slavers who sold their human cargo in the insatiable markets of the Persian Gulf and on the Indian subcontinent. Ranavalona was incensed by the British embargo, and so too were the white planters of the islands of Mauritius and Reunion. These men had benefited greatly from a ready supply of captives to work in their cane plantations, and it was estimated that these two islands alone possessed a combined slave population of over 20,000 souls. Despite a threatened insurrection on Mauritius, the British government stood firm, the slave trade remained illegal, and both Ranavalona and the planters were forced to accommodate themselves to this new restrictive situation.

Taken together, these three events simply reinforced Ranavalona's suspicion and hatred of foreigners, and produced a big change in her attitude towards her Christian subjects. In December 1834 she again withdrew her former tolerance of the Christians. An order was issued from the palace that forbade anyone from learning to read or write in the mission schools; from that time, only those schools established by the government were permitted to teach. But this prohibition was merely a foretaste of Ranavalona's coming wrath.

In 1835 the queen turned the screw a little more. In the middle of February the noble Ritsimanisa rose before the queen and publicly accused the Christians of sedition. They were, he said:

> changing the customs of the twelve sovereigns of Imerina. Of Andrianimpoinimerina, of Lehidama, and of Ranavalona-Manjaka. They despised the idols of the Queen, the Sikidy, and the customs of their forefathers; moreover, they were in league with the foreigners, and would transfer the kingdom to them.

Ranavalona listened calmly to this prearranged speech, then responded with an oath, swearing to prevent any and all such occurrences, and commanding that a grand *kabary* (meeting) should be assembled for the first day in March. Messengers were immediately sent out ordering all the headmen of every village of

Imerina to ensure that 'all who were able to walk, men, women, children and slaves' should attend the grand *kabary* on the plains of Mahamasima, to the west of the capital. None was excepted from the royal summons, save a single person from each household who might stay at home to ensure the safety of the property. By this the people knew the importance the queen attached to the coming conclave.

When the day of the *kabary* arrived, long lines of troops were in evidence and incessant cannon and musket fire served to underline the limitless power of the queen. She herself was not present at the assembly, and her message was conveyed to the masses by the capital's principal judge. The queen, he declared, had turned her face against the foreign religion. She called on 'all who had been baptised, who had worshipped and kept the sabbath, or entered into Christian society, to come forward and accuse themselves, and confess their *crimes* under pain of death'. The queen's prime minister-cum-lover, Rainiharo, then took the stand and warned all present that, unless the guilty parties came forward to profess their offence, he and other loyal members of the government were quite prepared to remove their impious heads.

News of the *kabary* sent waves of apprehension through the small community of missionaries at the capital. And within two weeks Ranavalona had increased the tension another notch, driving yet another nail into the coffin she was slowly constructing to bury, once and for all, the despised *vazah* religion. On February 26, Ratsimanisa and several Merina officers entered the chapel at Ambatonakanga (a district of the capital) and read aloud a letter from the queen addressed to the missionaries in which she forbade Christian baptism, religious worship or proselytising within her territories. Ranavalona made no attempt to prevent the Europeans from practising their own religion *themselves* – but she made it clear that any further attempts to convert any of her subjects to the Christian cause would result in very grave consequences indeed. In effect, Ranavalona had given notice to the missionaries that their services were no longer needed, that their work would not now be tolerated, anywhere in her realm.

As the news of the letter circulated the capital, Malagasy converts who had been attracted to the new religion out of a desire for the material benefits of European civilisation began to fall away. Many took advantage of the queen's offer to accuse themselves and confessed their former adherence to the foreign religion, at the same time offering cattle and money as self-imposed fines, and swearing that they would never again listen to the blandishments of the foreign priests. This, it seemed, was enough for the queen: she reduced in rank some former Christian teachers and army officers, with for example a Christian general (ten 'honours') degraded to a lieutenant (five 'honours'). In addition, around 2,000 citizens were made to pay a small fine; and she forced some of the more prominent members of Merina society to pay substantial monetary damages for their 'sin'. However, the bloody retribution that many feared simply did not materialise – or at least, not for the moment.

# CHAPTER ELEVEN

# Black Versailles

**D**espite Ranavalona's increasingly anti-Christian and anti-*vazah* stance, she simultaneously maintained a parallel obsessive, and apparently schizophrenic, admiration for all things European. Any snippet of information or engraving concerning Parisian haute couture was seized on avidly by the queen, and copies taken. No sooner had they made their appearance on the royal person than they would be imitated by the nobility, and 'accessorised' with singularly inappropriate adornments that would have brought tears to the eyes of their original designers. The problem was that the designs arrived in the capital piecemeal, some up to date, others fifty years old, with the result that the Antananarivo *beau monde* displayed a disconcerting melange of period crinolines, figure-hugging Empire-line dresses and contemporary fashion.

When a portrait of Marie Antoinette, with flowers adorning her ample wig, became known at the Imerina capital, the demand for artificial flowers rocketed. Laborde suggested using the beautiful flowers of the Malagasy forests as a substitute, but he was informed that the queen and her court were not savages – only synthetic blooms *à la Français* were acceptable. Not to be defeated, the inventive Gascon devised a method of manufacturing the required flowers and, lacking stems of brass, fastened the petals to shoots made from beaten rifle barrels. They were a sensation and, while the fashion lasted, were overindulged in recklessly, leading one account to describe the female members of the aristocracy, their hair thickly plastered with the blooms, as 'floral porcupines'.

With the industrial site (itself a mirror of European dynamism) up and running at Mantasoa, and the artificial flower supply secure, Ranavalona seems to have prevailed on Laborde to produce for her a Europe in miniature among the wooded mountains of the Merina highlands. How much this desire was abetted by homesickness on the part of the Frenchman it is difficult to say, but it is perhaps telling that the first building Laborde constructed, after his work at Mantasoa was completed, was not another palace for the queen but a new home for himself – a perfect stone-built replica of a Normandy farmhouse, thatched with reeds, with a huge central room and two adjoining wings. Spread out in front of the house and reached by a paved pathway, there was a typical French garden, burgeoning with lupins and roses, and planted with floral rings, stars and circles. At the centre was a large heart within which Laborde had planted purple flowers to form a double intertwined 'R', in honour of his patron, Ranavalona Regina. The farmhouse and gardens occupied a wonderful site among the mountains, set on a grassy hillock between two small lakes, and the building excited the admiration, and envy, of the Malagasy nobles fortunate enough to be invited to Laborde's retreat. Like all elites, they were constantly searching for something by which to mark themselves off from the hoi polloi, and soon everyone of note, including the queen, was aspiring to this new aspect of 'European chic'.

Laborde set to work with a will, giving himself the task of building an alternative capital where Ranavalona and her court could pass the dry season in peace and seclusion. And so, on a large hill overlooking the wooden huts of the Mantasoan workers, there arose what came to be called the Black Versailles, the incongruous spectacle of a stone-built town, with each dwelling constructed in various discordant European styles. Field

Marshal Coroller lived in the mansion he named 'Coeur Volant' ('flying heart'); close by was the 'Happy Few', the English-named house of the minister of foreign affairs. The queen's two native lovers, Rainiharo and Renijohary, had French-style houses named respectively 'Tendre Fougère' ('tender fern') and 'Rose Safranée' ('saffron rose'). Ranavalona herself preferred to dwell in a simple Swiss chalet that, hinting perhaps at her own desire for eternal youth, she named 'Soatsinranampiovana' ('immmutable beauty').

For all its simplicity, Ranavalona's chalet was surrounded by wide, carefully constructed gardens and walkways; one pathway led to a thickly wooded islet, at the centre of which Laborde had constructed a concrete swimming pool, with a marble throne and circular terracing. The water for the pool came not from the Varinah, the river that fed the dark forges and creaking waterwheels of Mantasoa, but from a hidden pipe that took its source, it was said, from seven sacred springs that rose high up in the mountain forest, and was perfumed by seven magical herbs. Each morning the court was in residence at the Black Versailles, Ranavalona would be carried out on the shoulders of her giant *tsimandao* to bathe in the pool, a long train of nobles, masseuses and slaves in her wake, and followed by a chorus of 200 female choristers, singing praises to the queen's wisdom and beauty. As she swam in the still waters, her court would surround the bathing place in strict order of precedence: princes, dukes and marquises were allowed to sit on the terracing around the pool, counts and viscounts disposed themselves on the lawns, while barons and the lesser orders were required to stand.

Afterwards, stretched out on her marble seat, Ranavalona would listen to the reports of her ministers of state while, at the same time, two Comoroan slaves attended on her. These bondswomen, who had studied the arts of beauty in the harem of the Sultan of Zanzibar, quietly and expertly ministered to her every need, drawing saffron rays of the sun around her navel, polishing her toes and applying violet paint, massaging her back, tapping her kidneys, and rubbing her knees and thighs with perfumed oil. On these occasions, it was said that she sometimes took much pleasure in employing the services of an Ethiopian slave, whose speciality was to trim the tresses of the royal pudenda with his teeth.

As the author of the Black Versailles, Jean Laborde continued to enjoy the favour of the queen and the many privileges he had been granted by her. But the Gascon was a worried man. Alongside the queen's appetite for things European was a mounting passion for cruelty; more and more she seemed to delight in the suffering of others. Despite the many advantages he himself received, Laborde was becoming increasingly concerned with Ranavalona's growing paranoia and indifference to the annihilation of her subjects. Thousands were being worked to death each year; she was commanding the *tanguena* ordeal for the most trivial offences, or simply on a whim, and those failing the test were being removed by ever more bestial methods of execution. Her newest conceit had been a horrendous variation on a long-standing demand that her subjects kiss or lick her feet when she gave them audience, as a sign of obeisance to her rule. Those suspected of Christian tendencies, helping the *vazah* or any of myriad real or imagined offences would find that the royal feet were not a normal colour, but instead bright pink. Refusal to kiss the queen's feet was treason, punishable by instant death; but licking the pink-coated toes was equally fatal, for they had been carefully dusted with poison. Laborde might be a favourite of the queen, but in Ranavalona's present paranoid frame of mind he must have wondered if it was only a matter of time before he found himself fatally close to the royal presence.

Yet it was also true that he was doing extremely well for himself at Antananarivo, amassing a fortune from the monopolies granted him by the queen. And the work of his industrial complex at Mantasoa made him an invaluable asset to both Ranavalona and the Merina nation. However, Laborde was still, in theory at least, a slave of the queen, a member of one of the lowest castes in Merina society. That made her decision to appoint him 'tutor' to Prince Rakota, her only child, all the more inexplicable.

In the normal course of events, the young prince could have expected to have been coached and instructed in his duties by an older member of the blood royal or, in any event, by a respected individual well versed in the Hova traditions. Other, lesser members of the royal line had, it was true, been given an immersion in European culture and technology, but for the education of the heir apparent to be entrusted to a foreigner was quite literally unprecedented. Laborde, however, took to his new post and responsibilities (which were additional to his duties at Mantasoa) with all his usual enormous enthusiasm, infusing his young charge with a lifelong appreciation of all things French. He spent all his free time with the boy, playing with him and teaching him with as much love, interest and tolerance as if he had been his own son; which, if the rumours sweeping Antananarivo at the time were true, perhaps he was.

The royal records give Rakoto's birth date as 1829, and his father is acknowledged as King Radama of the Merina. The latter claim is demonstrably untrue, as Radama died in 1828, more than nine months before the boy's birth. Or at least it is untrue according to our western scientific lights. Strangely, in nineteenth-century Madagascar, it was the custom that 'When a man dies ... any children his widow may afterwards have, are looked upon as his'. It has long been assumed that Rakoto's biological father must have been one of Ranavalona's early lovers. Given the date of his birth, this was most likely the brave but tragic Andrianmihaja, who helped Ranavalona to the throne and then died so valiantly, refusing the *tanguena* ordeal and coolly instructing the executioner on the exact spot through which to drive the killing blow. But is this date correct?

There may have been important reasons of state driving the obfuscation of Prince Rakoto's true birth date, which could well have been altered for reasons of dynastic convenience. The prince was known to have a strong rival for the throne in the form of his cousin Prince Rambosalama, a young man of undoubted royal descent, who at one period had been the official heir to the Merina throne. At that time Ranavalona had been well into middle age, and few had believed that the queen was capable of conceiving so close to the end of her reproductive life. It seems that Ranavalona shared this opinion, for it was she who had chosen Rambosalama, a favourite nephew, as her official heir. As might be expected, Rambosalama grew quickly into this new role. Within a very short period he had assumed all the airs and graces of a crown prince, lording it over the remaining princes of the blood in the confident expectation of his accession to the throne, just as soon as his formidable aunt had passed from the scene. Then came Ranavalona's unanticipated pregnancy and the birth of her son, Rakoto. With the unfeeling thoughtlessness of a true autocrat, Ranavalona discarded her erstwhile heir: Rambosalama was summarily demoted, and had to content himself once again with the status of mere 'prince'. It was a condition he was not prepared to accept without a fight.

Given the question marks over the paternity of the new heir, Rambosalama may have felt himself entirely justified in refusing to bow to the will of the queen. Whatever the reasons, he had quickly surrounded himself with supporters and, by contrasting his own belief in the ancient customs with that of Rakoto's francophile tendencies, his support had grown considerably. In addition, being one of the richest of the nobility, he had been able to secure even greater support by the careful distribution of honours and bribes. The result was that the Merina elite was now divided into two powerful opposing camps, Rakoto's 'modernisers' and Rambosalama's 'reactionaries', with the latter probably in the majority. The queen's natural son, and new heir, needed to acquire as much legitimacy as possible.

With King Radama cited as Rakoto's 'official' sire, and his biological father generally acknowledged as Andrianmihaja (himself of noble blood), Ranavalona's son would be seen as at least as legitimate a claimant as his rival, and the queen could be reasonably confident of a trouble-free transition of power to her son once she vacated the throne. But should the true father have been a foreigner, and a white slave to boot, Rakoto's chances of retaining the sceptre could only have been severely diminished. Despite the deified nature of Ranavalona's own bloodline, Rakoto would undoubtedly have been regarded as of inferior stock by the common people, especially when contrasted with the 'pure descent' of Rambosaloma. It may be, then, that Jean Laborde, Ranavalona's 'white bull', played along with this subterfuge as the only way to protect his son, the fruit of his affair with the queen.

There is much to commend this theory. According to the official account Rakoto was born just a few months after Radama died; yet a contemporary of the prince mentions that 'he was born long after King Radama's death'. Again, the relationship between Jean Laborde and the prince was undeniably intense, and far deeper than the simple friendship that might be expected to arise between tutor and pupil. The perceptive and indomitable lady traveller, Ida Pfeiffer, visited Madagascar in 1857, towards the end of Ranavalona's reign. She stayed for several weeks at the capital and was able to observe at first hand the bond between the prince and his mentor. On one occasion she was having dinner with Laborde when Prince Rakoto paid an unexpected visit:

> *The two men held each other in a long embrace, but for some time neither of them could find a word to express his joy. It was easy to see that a deep and true friendship existed between them.*

Perhaps most telling of all, those few Europeans who met the prince almost invariably commented on his distinctly European appearance. Ida Pfeiffer wrote that the prince was

> *short of stature, and his face does not betray a likeness, in form or colour, to any of the four races that inhabit Madagascar. His features have quite the type of the Moldavian Greek ... [and] he often goes about in European costume.*

Indeed, it was obvious from the first that Prince Rakoto possessed a distinct partiality to France, Jean Laborde's native land.

Taken together, we can be forgiven for suspecting strongly that the future heir to the Merina throne was in all probability Laborde's son. Certainly, many in Madagascar believed this to be true, and greatly resented the 'fact' that a foreigner would in time rule over them and perhaps hand the nation over to the hated *vazah*. It was a suspicion that was to have the most tragic consequences.

# CHAPTER TWELVE

# An Embassy to Europe

During the course of 1835, following the queen's clampdown on Christian worship, four of the six English missionaries, Cameron, Freeman, Chick and Kitching, decided to quit Madagascar, leaving behind just two of their number David Johns and Edward K. Baker. Many of their joint achievements had been ruined by Ranavalona's 'quiet persecution' of Christianity: the schools were closed and most of their converts had, through fear of reprisals, returned to the worship of the traditional gods. But not all was lost – the missionaries did leave behind them a small number of Christian 'cells', groups of committed co-religionists who worshipped in secret and at night, in rural retreats or deep in the forest to escape detection. And just before they departed, they had the satisfaction of seeing the first copies of the Bible roll off the press they had brought from England, a Bible printed in the native tongue of the Merina. The two missionaries who remained in the capital did not long outstay their brethren; they remained only to complete the preparation and printing of the first Malagasy–English dictionary. With that task accomplished (and having secretly distributed Christian literature and a sizeable number of Bibles to the faithful), Johns and Baker took ship for England.

It is a measure of the vindictiveness felt by the queen that, as each group of missionaries left her realm, their servants were arrested and immediately given the *tanguena* ordeal. Several of these wretches failed the test and were executed without delay by the usual barbarous methods. It was yet another indication of the queen's xenophobia and her increasing determination to have as little as possible to do with the outside world. But just as the missionaries were preparing to depart an incident took place that made the queen and her advisers question the wisdom of their anti-Christian policy.

The whole Merina economy was underpinned by a single annual event – the sending forth, during the dry season, of predatory military expeditions against other Madagascan tribes. Such raids brought back the wealth, in the form of booty, livestock and slaves, that alone sustained the prominence of the Merina over the rest of the Great Red Island. The soldiers conducting these incursions were expected to see to their own provisioning when in the field, so that, even when travelling through friendly areas, the havoc wreaked by tens of thousands of armed men forcibly seizing whatever they desired was incalculable. Taking their cue from the Merina army's piratical ways, many of the inhabitants of these devastated villages fled to the mountains and forests and adopted a life of brigandage, to such an extent that it was impossible to travel the roads and highways without an armed guard for protection.

During 1835 the problem became so great that a considerable military force was sent into the forest and succeeded in capturing around 200 of these reluctant robbers. They were brought back to the capital where they were

*publicly executed, 84 were killed by the spear, 17 were burnt alive, some were buried alive and the rest, having been declared guilty by the tanguena, were killed on the spot. By these sanguinary measure the Government sought to deter the people from endeavouring to escape from their requirements.*

Such 'police actions' did not prevent the bulk of the army from engaging in its annual excursion of pillage and rapine. One expedition was sent under the command of Rainiharo against the still-unsubdued Sakalava clans around St Augustine's Bay. It consisted of upwards of 10,000 warriors, with bearers and camp followers swelling that number threefold. They proceeded through the land of their 'allies' the Betsileo like a swarm of locusts, killing as they marched and stripping the land bare of provisions. Moving slowly across the island, the army reached Sakalava territory, only to find that their enemy refused to give battle, and were content instead to mount lightning raids against the slow-moving, cumbersome Merina forces, and then to melt away again into the safety of the forests.

Frustrated and dispirited, Rainiharo sent several thousand men under the command of Rainingory, an officer of the 11th honour, to secure the port in Isalary, and to sack the surrounding villages whose inhabitants were suspected of aiding and supplying the Sakalava insurgents. Unfortunately, when he arrived at the port Rainingory was faced with the imposing sight of twenty-one European vessels, all formidable three-masters, at anchor in the bay. Believing that this naval flotilla would take exception to the destruction he had been ordered to visit upon the port and its surrounding villages, Rainingory lost all stomach for a fight and led his men back in an ignominious rout to the main body of the Merina army. The expedition then abandoned the campaign, and attempted to return to Antananarivo; but they were travelling back along the route by which they had previously advanced, through a region they themselves had destroyed utterly. Without the usual captured livestock and grains to sustain them the soldiers suffered terribly, and thousands lost their lives to starvation. One English observer gave a graphic description of a similar march by men whose army was totally bereft of even the most primitive commissariat:

> *I cannot paint the situation of the Ovas [Merina]. They are covered with dirt, half-starved, half-drowned and naked. They eat anything they can get without cooking.*

The irony was that, had Rainingory looked just a little closer at the ships in Isalary Bay, he might have seen that the vessels of the 'naval flotilla' posed no threat whatsoever to the Merina army. They were, in fact, American whalers that had fetched up at the port in search of water and provisions.

But the presence of this misidentified 'foreign fleet' was to have even greater repercussions than the defeat of a Merina incursion and the saving of a few Sakalava villages. When the disturbing news was brought to the capital by the remnants of the returning army, it served as a forceful reminder to Ranavalona and her advisers of their vulnerability to European sea power. None of the Merina nobles was under any illusions about the ultimate strategy of the *vazah*: both Britain and France desired and planned for a compliant Madagascar, the French via outright conquest and colonisation, the British – at the moment at least – through a pervasive and guiding influence on the island's ruling elite. If either of these foreigners obtained their goal, Merina independence and pre-eminence would be gone forever.

Nor was it lost on them that many of King Radama's victories over the coastal tribes had been aided and abetted by *vazah* ships. But this foreign aid was a two-edged sword: it could just as easily be withdrawn and placed at the disposal of the enemies of Imerina, as the presence of the twenty-one warships in Isalary Bay implied. Were the foreigners angry at the restrictions placed on their missionaries and the persecution visited on the Malagasy converts? Was it, perhaps, time to placate the *vazah* with promises and honeyed words? It would cost nothing and might achieve much.

Ranavalona certainly believed that such a policy could advance the Merina cause, and in the summer of 1836 the queen commanded that an embassy of six officers be sent from Madagascar to England and to France. Its primary objective was damage limitation, but Ranavalona also hoped to persuade the French to accept her as Queen of Madagascar, a title that, hitherto, they had steadfastly refused to grant.

The ambassadors were led by the prince Adriantsitohaina and had two secretaries in attendance. The delegation travelled to Europe aboard the French ship of the line *Mathilde*. They carried letters to the King of England and the King of France expressing friendship and a desire for trade, but there was no specific motivation for the visit beyond a rather vague desire to mitigate any military response that the queen's blatantly xenophobic policy might engender (the memory of the twenty-one-ship 'naval flotilla' at Isalary remained a potent symbol of European sea power, and a source of great concern, to Ranavalona).

The reception of the embassy in both France and England was undertaken with every attention to diplomatic protocol. Britain was the first port of call, and the Merina ambassadors were taken on a whistle-stop tour of the country's many wonders, with the intention of demonstrating Britain's superiority in both military and industrial terms, and the benefits of trading with so great a power. In parallel with this, they met the directors of the London Missionary Society, who impressed on them the importance of a resumption of Christian teaching, which they claimed was the basis of Britain's success in the world. The ambassadors also had an audience with King William IV and were invited to a reception at Windsor Castle. The meeting apparently went well, though Queen Adelaide's request that the embassy should 'tell the Queen of Madagascar from me, that she can do nothing so beneficial for her country as to receive the Christian religion' can hardly have endeared European royalty to Ranavalona, and once again demonstrates the almost unbridgeable chasm in cultural perceptions that existed between the two societies.

At a number of meetings, Lord Palmerston suggested a new Anglo-Malagasy treaty, which would incorporate much of the old 1817 and 1820 concordats between Britain and King Radama, and would have allowed for the exchange of consuls and for unlimited access to Madagascar for British traders and missionaries. This was too much for the ambassadors – they had been given only limited authority to treat with foreign governments – and the embassy left for France without agreeing to anything.

The French response to their visitors was an extremely civil and diplomatic non-response. The embassy was received with all honour and due deference, but the French had not abandoned their scheme to subdue Ranavalona's kingdom, and wanted to discover if the Queen of the Hova (they never granted Ranavalona the title she sought, Queen of Madagascar) would acquiesce to their plans for the island. Like the British, they soon discovered that the embassy did not possess the authority to negotiate – as the ambassadors apologetically explained, all they could offer was to report back to the Great Glory on their return to Madagascar, after which her response would be forwarded to the French authorities 'in due course'. This was simply not good enough, and the French lost all interest in their visitors. The Malagasies were given the sop of a dinner with Emperor Louis-Philippe then hurriedly hussled aboard ship and transported back to Madagascar on the *Mathilde*. As a forlorn hope, the French authorities appointed the captain of the vessel, Andrew Garnot, to carry their own proposals to Antananarivo and seek audience with Ranavalona. If she was amenable, all well and good; but should she prove intransigent, the French had other plans to obtain a toehold on the island.

CHAPTER THIRTEEN

# The Persecutions Begin

**C**aptain Garnot followed the Merina embassy through the Malagasy lowlands to Antananarivo. It was not the most opportune time to visit. The embassy's report to the queen made it obvious that the aims of the mission had not been achieved, and the monarch's anger was terrible to see. Captain Garnot tried to make the best of a bad situation, putting forward the French government's proposals for political and commercial intercourse in as favourable a light as possible, but without success. His ideas were rejected in toto,

> and the proceedings of the Hova officials showed that they were desirous of terminating the influence of all Europeans, without respect to any particular nationality, in the island, and were determined to pertinaciously repel the slightest attempt of any foreign surveillance or control.

It seems that Ranavalona was now feeling far less insecure, as this same year the first judicial murders of Christians began. Up until this time the queen had left the Christian converts to their own devices, believing that, with the foreign missionaries departed, the sect would simply die out. Instead, to her consternation and annoyance, interest in the Europeans' religion had continued to increase. To stem the tide, an example had to be made.

The choice fell on fourteen Christians, several of whom had previously fallen foul of the queen by refusing to obey her command to return to the worship of the old gods. All were arrested and condemned to death, but at the last moment the sentence was commuted to one of perpetual slavery, and they were allotted separately to the households of various nobles in the capital. It seems that even this cruel fate did nothing to dim the religious ardour of many of the converts, and one, a woman named Rasalama, was heard declaring her continued belief in Christ and her readiness to accept martyrdom. When this was declared to the queen and her advisers, the result was inevitable. Whipped and loaded down with chains, Rasalama was dragged through the streets of the capital the next morning, singing her Christian hymns, and was taken outside the city to Ambohipotsy, the hill of death. There, after begging for, and obtaining, the chance to make a last prayer to her God, she was speared to death.

It may be that the intransigence of Ranavalona and her government, and her willingness to kill native converts of the foreign religion, was not so much a display of confidence as a posture of defiance. With the embassy to Europe revealing that neither Britain nor France was prepared to deal on terms acceptable to Ranavalona, there was now no reason for reining in those anti-Christian, xenophobic forces that simmered both in the majority of the populace and within the queen's own psyche. Laborde's factories gave her an additional advantage: uniquely among native kingdoms facing European colonial expansion, Ranavalona was totally self-sufficient in terms of guns and gunpowder, and this would allow the Merina to fight the Europeans on something like equal terms. If the *vazah* were so obviously intent on gaining control of the Great Red Island, the Merina's best strategy for maintaining their own dominion was one of total disengagement and the securing of the nation's borders. Ideally, as much of the coast as possible should be taken into Merina hands, in order to deny the Europeans the chance of gaining a bridgehead on the island, especially in any region close to the capital.

With this in mind, Ranavalona attempted to take control of any areas adjoining her realm that were not yet under her authority. Prime among these were the northern territory of the Sakalava and some of the western plain, where small independent tribes still held out against her rule.

She first sent her forces against the northern Sakalava, who the year before had used fabian tactics to fight an earlier Merina expedition to a standstill, with both sides sustaining heavy casualties. The Sakalava were led by Andriantsolo, a charismatic and accomplished chieftain who, knowing the Merina dread of seafaring, had availed himself of a fortified island sanctuary at Nosy Faly, to which he retired whenever the queen's forces pressed him too hard and from which he launched his own raids deep into Merina territory, at times approaching within a few days of Antananarivo and threatening the capital itself.

This time it would be different. The queen was determined to annihilate this troublesome foe – whose obstinate resistance was kindling the fires of rebellion in other subject people – with a display of overwhelming force. In the summer of 1837, Ranavalona sent an army of more than 12,000 warriors and bearers against the Sakalava chieftain. But the plan went badly adrift. The proud Merina army

> *was completely defeated, many of the officers and troops killed, and the remnant of the expedition returned in disgrace to the capital without having accomplished their object.*

Notwithstanding this ignominious reverse, Ranavalona immediately began planning for a second expedition, larger than the last, to take the field during the following campaign season.

Faced with the prospect of continual warfare with a foe superior in numbers and equipment, Andriantsolo and the rest of the autonomous tribes of the north-west coast cast about anxiously for help. The realisation that by themselves they could not forever withstand the annual despoliation of their country by the Merina army brought them to desperate measures, and they finally made overtures to the French governor of Reunion, the unfortunately named Contre-Amiral de Hell. This was the opportunity the French had been seeking. De Hell began negotiations with these independent groups, dangling before them the prospect of French protection from Ranavalona's constant depredations. All that was required to obtain this happy state of affairs was for the chieftains to cede their land as a French protectorate. The negotiations continued over 1839 and into 1840, and were crowned with success for de Hell, who provisionally accepted the native concessions, pending confirmation from Paris. This was swiftly given, and over the next year Tsihomaiko, Queen of Iboina, Tsimiaro, King of Ankaran Province, and the redoubtable Andriantsolo, chief of Nosy Faly, all signed conventions ceding their land to the French government.

But the French remained cautious; despite their promise of succour for all who ceded their dominions, under pressure from the Chambers the government of Louis-Philippe chose to declare only the islands around the coast as French possessions. These were the very areas that required no protection, and that the native tribes could easily have defended themselves. The king, queen and chieftain who had handed over their lands to the French were forced to watch helpless as Ranavalona's army returned to attack the coastal lands with impunity, 'massacring without pity those who resisted, and forcing their odious yoke of servitude on the provinces of Iboina and Ankarana'.

No matter: the French government had what it wanted – a secure foothold on Madagascar. And so too did the Catholic

Queen Ranavalona.

Madagascan warriors.

Radama II with crown.

Scenic of the capital showing the Great Palace.

Village with missionary in litter.

Ida Pfeiffer.

Ida Pfeifer, Laborde and others during their 'trial' before the queen.

Great *kabary* at Antananarivo.

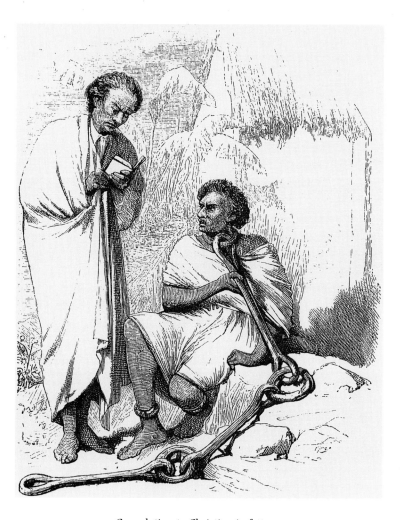

Consolation to Christian in fetters.

Church. No sooner had Monsieur Passot taken possession of the island of Nosy Be in the name of France than a missionary, the Abbé Dalmond, had set himself up on the new colony (the Abbé had, in fact, been present during the negotiations that led to the ceding of the region, acting as interpreter between M Passot and Queen Tsihomaiko, and had lost no time in staking his own claim to the souls of the islanders). Before he could properly begin his ministry he was recalled to Reunion, but quickly returned, bringing with him three priestly companions, Messieurs Joly, Minot and Tarroux, all equally zealous in their desire to bring the word of God to the Malagasy.

The Abbé Joly was placed on the old French possession of Ile Ste Marie, and the other three priests repaired to Tafondro on the island of Nosy Be, where they quickly built a chapel and a school and began the work of saving souls. It must have appeared that their new ministry was blessed with good fortune, but after this auspicious beginning things went rapidly downhill.

At the same time that the priests were establishing themselves on Nosy Be, the French frigate *La Dordogne* arrived at the island, disembarking over a hundred troops who set up camp close to the priests, on the coastal strip that lay beneath the mountain of Lokobe. The soldiers called their settlement 'Hell-Ville' in honour of Contre-Amiral de Hell, who had led the negotiations that obtained the island for France, but the name of their camp soon took on (to English ears at least) a far more sinister connotation. Lying next to the coastal swamps, Hell-Ville was plagued with mosquitoes and very soon malarial fever exploded in the camp, carrying off at least eighty of the troops within a few days. The French had learned a hard lesson. As a later report emphasised:

> It is therefore essential, before attempting anything of importance against Madagascar, to identify what are, on the coast, the most salubrious points, those where it is possible to establish ourselves without having our soldiers run the risk of being poisoned.

Abbé Dalmond was in for a further shocking reverse. Tsimiaro, the King of Nosy Mitsio and the former King of Ankarana

Province – now subsumed into Ranavalona's 'empire' – had apparently thought better of his bargain with the French. Disgusted by their refusal to honour the pledge of protection he had been given, King Tsimiaro had embraced Islam and withdrawn to the one small portion of his former kingdom that the French would defend, the island of Nosy Mitsio. When the good abbé attempted to demonstrate to the king the error of his ways and draw him back into the Christian fold, he revealed all the militant intolerance of the newly converted, threatening the priest's life with such vehemence that Abbé Dalmond was quickly faced with a choice between flight and imminent martyrdom. The Frenchman decided to delay the delights of paradise. He left the island, never to return, and quickly made sail for his base at Nosy Be.

Here he discovered no better news: two of his priestly companions had been rendered *hors de combat* by a most virulent strain of malaria that left them too weak to continue their ministry. The third, M Minot, seems to have suffered from an early form of culture shock: he had done little since his arrival and had even refused to learn the Malagasy language, without which his presence as a missionary was superfluous. Sad at heart, the four missionaries decided to abandon Madagascar, and just a few weeks later sailed for the safety of the French colony on Reunion. Only the Abbé Dalmond's evangelising spirit remained undimmed, and from Reunion the ever-resourceful cleric sailed for France in 1843, returning the following year with six members of the Company of Jesus. This time, despite hardship and many dangers (and the complete failure of their mission at St Augustine's Bay), the Jesuits managed to establish themselves on Nosy Be, where they remained, a small nucleus of Catholicism in a hostile world, awaiting better times.

# CHAPTER FOURTEEN

# The Buffalo Hunt

For Ranavalona and her government, the news of the French reverses in the north-west were greeted with rejoicing. Flushed with the booty and slaves from the successful expedition to subdue the provinces of Iboina and Ankarana, the queen's morale was high and the nation itself felt ready to take on all-comers. There was no appetite for change, no reason to accommodate Merina society even partially to the norms of behaviour accepted by the 'civilised' West. And so matters continued within the queen's domains as they had always done, a situation described by one historian as

> *constant persecution of religious sects, rigorous exclusion of foreigners from the interior and coast, annual military expeditions, executions and exactions; cruel oppression and misery everywhere.*

For her part, Ranavalona was happy to allow matters to return to normal at Antananarivo. Her victory gave her time to enjoy one of the traditional recreations of royalty, the buffalo hunt. In 1845 she made a progress to the outlying district of Manerinerina to enjoy the pleasures of the chase. But this was to be no intimate hunting party: the queen commanded the entire court to accompany her on her journey, and in order to make as impressive a progress as possible, each noble was required to bring his household and his slaves with him. The result was that upwards of 50,000 people marched with the queen, including 10,000 soldiers and an equal number of bearers.

The advance of such a great host was extremely slow, especially as, in accordance with her dead husband's will, Ranavalona had allowed no roads to be constructed in any part of her domain (King Radama had believed that such paved highways would aid the advance of any invader). But the queen's dignity prevented her from travelling on the simple tracks of the peasantry, so Ranavalona commanded that a road be built for her *as she progressed*. Twelve thousand men were forced into its construction, digging ditches, cutting down forests, moving boulders and clearing bush, working at a crippling pace so that the completed road was always one day's journey ahead of the royal party. As if this were not enough, Ranavalona commanded that other workers, and their families, were sent forward to build an entire small town, complete with a high surrounding rampart of earth, for each of her nightly stops.

Such a commission would have tried the competence of any army or engineer, but the queen demanded all these operations with no thought for the logistics required. There was no commissariat to organise supplies or sanitary arrangements for the court. The 50,000 who followed the royal train were expected to shift for themselves when it came to food. As a result, once the provisions they could carry ran out, the whole throng simply descended on the closest towns and villages and carried off whatever supplies they could find. Destruction and famine followed in the wake of the royal progress, and as the outing lasted a full four months, even the nobles following the royal train were soon reduced to starvation, with huge prices being paid for even the smallest quantity of rice.

The condition of the road makers was even more deplorable. Once again, no provision was made for their upkeep and they were simply worked until they dropped, at which time more of Her Majesty's loyal subjects were pressed into service. The royal road was littered with corpses, most of which were not even buried, but simply thrown into some convenient ditch or under a nearby bush. In total, 10,000 men, women and children are said to have perished during the sixteen weeks of the queen's 'hunt'. In all this time, there is no record of a single buffalo being shot.

In this climate of triumph and omnipotence, Ranavalona's *hauteur*, her belief in her own supremacy over ordinary mortals, reached new heights. She was no longer prepared to accept any abuse of her laws by foreigners. In March 1845, Captain Jacob Heppick fell foul of the Female Caligula when he attempted to abduct seven of her subjects, whom he had lured on board his ship before ordering the vessel made ready for the open sea. But the Malagasy abductees were too quick for him and escaped ashore to raise the alarm. It must be said that Captain Heppick, an American-born British subject, was in all probability the guilty party in this incident – he almost certainly intended selling the seven natives abroad as slaves or indentured labourers. However, the tables were quickly turned and the justice exacted barbaric, if not somewhat poetic. Heppick was arrested by the Merina authorities, bound in chains, and held in confinement for several weeks. Eventually, the would-be slaver was put on trial, found guilty and condemned to slavery for life. He was put up for sale at public auction and would no doubt have ended his days after a life of servitude somewhere in the interior had he not been purchased by his friends at the last moment.

The Heppick incident acted as a catalyst for Ranavalona, convincing her of the need for stern action against the *vazah*. Apart from this, she was especially incensed by the cavalier attitude of a number of European merchants, who had set up their factories on the east coast and were trading there in defiance of monopoly rights granted by Ranavalona to de Lastelle and certain members of the queen's entourage. Several of the incomers had even established cane plantations on her territory, selling sugar not only to Mauritius and Bourbon, but even to her own capital Antananarivo. While she had continued to believe that her position vis-à-vis the foreigners was one of weakness, Ranavalona had felt obliged to tolerate their excesses – but no longer.

She began turning the screw by increasing the cost of cattle exported to the islands of Mauritius and Reunion for meat (an imposition that hurt the beef-loving British far more than the French). By the middle of 1844 the price demanded per bullock was fifteen Spanish dollars, almost twice the eight dollars demanded just a few weeks earlier. Compounding this, she enacted a law that prevented Malagasy labourers from working on the sugar plantations on these islands, an edict that struck an effective blow at the economy of the islands and at French and British colonial income.

Then, on May 13, 1845, less than two months after Jacob Heppick had been arrested, all the inhabitants of Tamatave, including the foreign traders, were suddenly ordered to attend a meeting at the home of Philibert, the chief judge of the town. Here they found the full Merina garrison of the fort in attendance, some 150 armed men, who surrounded the traders while a proclamation from the queen was read out across the heads of the assembled throng. To general shock and consternation, the twelve British and eleven French traders heard that, from this day forth, all privileges granted to the foreigners were revoked and all would be subject to Malagasy law. They would be required

> to perform all the corvées of the Queen, to be put on the public
> works the same as slaves, to take the tanguena ordeal whenever
> the law obliged, to be sold and made slaves if they were in debt, to
> obey all the Merina officers, to have no prerogatives more than

*any other Malagasy subjects, not to leave Tamatave on any*
*pretext, and to have no commerce with the interior of the island.*

They were, in effect, ruined. Fifteen days were given to the traders
to either accede to the new law or to see their houses and factories
invaded by the mob, their merchandise looted, and they
themselves placed on whatever ship first entered Tamatave
harbour. The queen was determined on their expulsion from the
island, and over the next four days the Merina authorities spared
no effort to menace and threaten the *vazah* at every turn.

Into this gathering storm now sailed a joint French and English
squadron of warships, the frigate HMS *Conway* commanded by
Captain Kelly, and two French ships under Commodore Bomain
Desfosses, *Le Berceau* and *La Zelée*. At the outset of the queen's
ultimatum the European traders had sent an appeal for protection to their respective governments, and in a rare example of
Franco-British colonial cooperation, the three ships had been sent
by Sir William Gomm, governor of Mauritius, and his Gallic
counterpart on Reunion, M Bazoche, to stabilise the situation at
Tamatave. Their orders were to attempt a reconciliation between
the traders and the queen's government 'by amicable means if
possible, but if not, by force of arms'.

Amicable negotiation proved impossible. Hamstrung by their
monarch's uncompromising proclamation, the Merina authorities
were intransigent and refused any concessions to the traders or to
the representatives of the British and French navies. An ultimatum
was delivered by Captain Kelly and Commodore Desfosses, and as
a precaution, all the remaining traders and their folk were taken
aboard the European vessels. The Merina's defiant response was
to sack and loot the traders' surviving homes and factories. On
their own responsibility the joint commanders of the naval force
decided on a punitive expedition as soon as the ultimatum
expired. They would bombard Tamatave, mount an amphibious
landing, take the town and the fort that defended it from the
Merina garrison, and burn the lot. The Sanguinary Queen would
learn the cost of defying the European powers.

No doubt Captain Kelly and Commodore Desfosses envisaged the action as a repeat of the successful French onslaught against Tamatave some 16 years earlier in 1829, when the enemy forces were defeated without the loss of a single French combatant. In the event, the assault did prove astonishingly similar to one of the French attacks against the Merina in 1829 – the disastrous offensive against Foule Point that same year.

The action started well enough, with the warships sending broadside after broadside into the town and the fort, and being answered in kind from the Merina batteries (both French ships lost topmasts during the exchange of fire). Longboats carried the invading Europeans to the beach under heavy fire and they formed up, 100 French and 250 British sailors and marines, and immediately raced across the sand to attack the external wooden palisade of the fort. The white and striped jerseys of matelot and tar mixed in a wild melee as they carried the outer defences with cutlass, pistol and the point of the bayonet, spiking the enemy's guns and rushing onwards, cheering triumphantly, towards the central keep. Here, just as at Foule Point so many years before, they discovered that the rough wooden outerworks obscured a far more formidable defensive structure than they had first imagined, a circular stone bastion with walls ten metres high, bristling with thirty guns and filled with defiant Merina warriors. Here the Franco-British attack wavered and died. Without adequate scaling ladders, with no means of breaching the wall, and taking substantial casualties from the well-placed shots of the enemy gunners, the officers had no option but to order the landing party to abandon the assault and retire in as good order as the chaotic situation allowed.

The aggressors carried with them a single trophy as they left the scene of battle, the castle's ensign, a flag bearing the word Ranavalona-Manjaka. It was an object that took on all the iconic character of a Roman legion's eagle, and quickly precipitated an incident that, in its tragi-comic effects, symbolised the jingoistic, colonial ardour of the Victorian age. The flag had originally been flown boldly on the outer palisade of the fort, from which it was shot away by allied fire, only to be picked up by a Merina soldier and fastened to his spear. It fell again and was seized by a British midshipman, who was almost immediately attacked by several Frenchmen, jealous of the British prize and intent on securing the flag for the honour of French arms. A scrimmage ensued, with the flag the centre of a tug-of-war between the erstwhile allies, who continued this battle-within-a-battle apparently oblivious of the Merina fire raining down on them. Several men were hit and badly injured during this exchange, and the matter was only resolved when one of the British officers, the Royal Navy's Lieutenant Kennedy, slashed at the flag, cutting it in two, leaving the French in possession of the half proclaiming 'Ranavalona' while the British received the 'Manjaka' portion of the pennant.

Honour apparently satisfied, the allies retreated to their longboats with fifty-five of their number wounded, including the resourceful Lieutenant Kennedy. They immediately weighed anchor and, still under fire from the victorious Merina fortifications, set sail for more friendly climes – the French to Reunion and the British to Mauritius – leaving behind on the beach seventeen French and four British dead.

It was never fully established why the allied dead were not brought off to the ships, which would have been normal practice during such an offensive operation. Possibly they were forgotten in the near panic that ensued when the strength of the Merina defensive position was fully realised, or perhaps it was simply the size and strength of the enemy counter-attack that precluded the removal of the dead. Whatever the reason, Queen Ranavalona's soldiery was not slow to utilise this opportunity to show its contempt for its 'defeated' foe. In an act that scandalised the European forces, the bodies of the twenty-one foreigners were decapitated and their heads fastened to poles placed all along the shoreline. They were to remain there for a further eight years, the flesh slowly falling from the skulls, swinging gently on the sea breezes and staring blindly out to sea, a warning to other insolent *vazah* who might think of violating the domain of the Great Glory.

# CHAPTER FIFTEEN

# The Great Conspiracy

**R**anavalona's response to the unsuccessful Anglo-French attack on Tamatave was immediate and had dire consequences for the allied island colonies in the Indian Ocean. At that time, both Reunion and Mauritius obtained almost their entire supply of beef from cattle raised on Madagascar and subsequently exported to the islands. The price had previously been almost doubled at the queen's command, causing great hardship on the islands. Now, she simply stopped the cattle trade completely.

Her timing was perfect, for at that moment a murrain or deadly plague was sweeping the island of Mauritius and had killed off most of the small stock of cattle being raised on the island. A great dearth of meat ensued, with the price of beef rocketing far above the previously unheard-of fifteen dollars. To make matters worse, the islanders had also become accustomed to importing chickens and a considerable proportion of their rice supply from Ranavalona's domains. These products, too, the queen embargoed.

The position of the British colonialists on Mauritius became so parlous that Governor Gomm wrote to the government in London beseeching the authorities there to dispatch an armed force capable of trouncing the proud queen and her army (which the British must by now have regretted both arming and training). But Lord Aberdeen, and later his successor Lord Palmerston, both refused to be drawn into any scheme for reprisals against Madagascar. For their part, the French were just as indignant at this reverse and at first, ignoring British reluctance to engage in retaliatory action, planned a large punitive expedition against Ranavalona under General Duvivier. But such was the political turmoil in the France of early 1846 that, while the French government was enthusiastic, the Chamber of Deputies steadfastly set their face against this new and risky adventure, and in the process 'sacrificed the honour of the country to a party victory'. In short, absolutely nothing was done: the British and French swallowed their pride, Mauritius and Reunion remained in a state of semi-starvation, and the Sanguinary Queen revelled in her ability to strike a blow against the encroaching Europeans with apparent impunity.

The Malagasy court did, in fact, expect a counter-stroke of some kind sooner or later, and preparations in the form of strengthened fortifications and defensive outworks were undertaken in a number of locations. But instead of armed troops, placatory messages arrived from the British and French *vazah* suggesting (but not demanding) a resumption of trade with the islands. Many Malagasy traders, including several noble families from the court at Antananarivo whose monopolies in imported produce had established their fortunes, were now suffering financially from the embargo on international trade. They too were keen for a normalisation of relations with the foreigners, so that they could once again avail themselves of this lucrative and regular income stream. But the queen remained unyielding in her pride. Her realm was a sovereign nation and the *vazah* had made an unprovoked attack on its shores – it was not in her nature simply to forgive and forget. She let it be known that she had no objection to a resumption of trade, provided the guilty parties in the recent hostilities were prepared to pay a fine of 15,000 *piastres* into the royal treasury.

So formal an admission of culpability stuck in the collective throats of the Europeans. Negotiations were terminated, and for the next few years the twenty-one *vazah* heads continued to swing on their posts at Tamatave, which, like all other ports on the Great Red Island, remained effectively closed to Franco-British shipping.

It was around this time that Jean Laborde became seriously alarmed by the increasing instability and xenophobia of the queen to whom he had devoted so many years of service. It had been his work, and his alone, that had given Ranavalona her own 'industrial revolution' (probably the first example of industrialisation outside of Europe and certainly unprecedented in Africa). His efforts had transformed Imerina from a tribal state into a self-sufficient 'nation', all but independent of European goods and armaments and hence immune to English or French diplomatic pressure. Laborde himself had grown phenomenally rich in the process, but it seems that he began to realise that he was a Frenchman first and only secondarily an independent trader and entrepreneur. Perhaps this had something to do with his advancing years and increasing longing for his home country; possibly the European heads at Tamatave and the queen's increasing paranoia led him to believe that it might only be a matter of time before his own head would come to grace a pole at one of the palaces that Laborde had so lovingly constructed for the Great Glory.

And in truth, the queen's behaviour did give grounds for concern. At a *kabary* to decide on actions to take to protect the island against foreign attack, either she or her counsellors had come up with three primary, and frankly insane, strategies. The first was to set up enormous iron shields close to coastal fortresses. Any cannonballs fired by enemy ships that hit these shields would then rebound from them, retracing their original trajectory and so sinking the aggressors. Should this cunning plan fail, a high wall was the next requirement, and this was to be built around the whole island, a distance of well over 5,000 kilometres. How the men and materiel were to be provided for this Brobdingnagian task was never explained.

But perhaps the most outlandish resolution to come from the great council was the suggestion to manufacture giant scissors as a defence against the enemy. Four of these enormous shears were to be constructed and placed – their blades left wide open – on the tracks leading from the four main ports to the capital. Any invader bold enough to have escaped the rebounding cannonades and then to have scaled the island-wide palisade would be snipped in two as he walked unsuspecting between the blades of this ingenious device.

That such ideas could be seriously discussed in royal conclave would justify anyone in doubting the sanity of those present. But whatever the root of his concern, it appears that Laborde became convinced of the need to break with his ruthless patron, to remove the Sanguinary Queen from her throne and to replace Ranavalona with a more civilised and less unstable ruler, preferably one whose inclinations would allow French interests to prosper. This was the beginning of the great conspiracy.

His choice fell, not unnaturally, on Rakoto, the queen's son, whose education had been entrusted for many years to his care, and of whom Laborde was, quite possibly, the father. Laborde was helped in this conspiracy by his old friend de Lastelle, the Creole planter who had first sent him, a destitute shipwrecked sailor and putative slave, to the court of the queen some fifteen years before. Together, they so worked on the mind of the young prince that he uncritically accepted their constant affirmations that Madagascar needed a powerful European nation to protect its interests in a hostile world.

At the time, Admiral Cecile of the French Navy was visiting Ile Ste Marie, on board the warship *Cleopatra*. Spurred on by the two French adventurers, Prince Rakoto was prevailed on to write a letter, requesting protection for his native land from 'la plus ancienne amie des peuples de Madagascar'. This missive was political dynamite, and while the naïve Rakoto may have missed its political significance, the two veteran Frenchmen can hardly have been ignorant of the momentous change this request would entail. By personal entreaty of the heir to the Merina throne, and in direct opposition to the wishes of the ruling monarch, the French were being asked to assume suzerainty over Madagascar. The country would cease to be an independent nation. The perpetrators of such a scheme must have known that, while she remained in power, Ranavalona would never have allowed her beloved nation, the legacy of Andrianampoinimerina and Radama, to bow to the yoke of any foreign 'protector'. The success of the scheme therefore demanded her removal.

It was treason, pure and simple.

Should news of the letter find its way to the queen, there was no knowing what her reaction might be. The *tanguena* ordeal was the least of the horrors that could await them. Laborde and de Lastelle had placed the prince, and themselves, in a most precarious and possibly fatal position.

But this momentous letter from Rakoto, which gave the perfect pretext for invasion and should by rights have galvanised Laborde's countrymen into action, was simply ignored. The French were still smarting from the bloody nose they had been given, along with the British, at Tamatave. European heads remained hanging from the posts there, and Ranavalona had refused to move on her original demand for a fine to compensate for the Franco-British attack. In short, at this point no one, least of all the French, was in the mood for another Madagascar adventure. Except for a missive from the French governor of Reunion expressing moral support and little else, the incriminating letter from Prince Rakoto was passed over, and the chance of establishing a French protectorate was allowed to lapse. Madagascar remained closed to European trade goods, and this first attempt at unseating the Sanguinary Queen came to nothing.

If European goods were no longer current in Madagascar, European religious ideas continued to circulate secretly at Imerina and to thrive. Planted so assiduously by the members of the London Missionary School prior to their expulsion, Christian ideals flourished and converts grew ever more numerous – and not simply among the downtrodden masses who might be expected to find a philosophy of 'rest after suffering' attractive. By 1848, several members of the aristocracy had also embraced the new faith, including four who traced their bloodline from the kingly stock. Even so high a personage as Prince Ramonja of the royal clan had accepted the tenets of the foreign creed. Christian worship was still an offence meriting terrible punishments, but while other converts remained vulnerable, Prince Ramonja's position, and that of the remaining nobility, was thought even by the Europeans to afford them a reasonable degree of safety.

All that changed one year later when Queen Ranavalona inaugurated yet another round of persecution against the Christian converts, intending on this occasion to destroy the hated foreign cult root and branch. No section of society was spared and over 2,000 men and women were arrested and put on trial for their lives, Prince Ramonja and the Christian nobles foremost among them. Many put up a spirited defence, denying that their beliefs made them traitors or in any way unfaithful to the queen or their country. One woman prisoner, who had taken the baptismal name of Mary, proclaimed that 'against the enemies of the Queen and her country the Christians will fight' and justified her refusal to worship the traditional fetish by explaining that

> *as for … the idols, and the mountains, God has not given them to be prayed unto; for they are things without life. But God is the*

*Lord of heaven and earth, and of all things; and for these reasons I
do not pray to things without life.*

Another young woman, Raniva, a noblewoman and a favourite
of the queen, fearlessly denied the power of the idols:

*God alone will I serve as long as my life shall last, for God has
given me life and spirit, a higher spiritual life to worship Him,
and for that reason I worship God.*

Ranavalona remained unmoved. Despite such protestations, all
the accused were found guilty and ordered to await the queen's
pleasure the following day.

Dawn came with a cannonade that continued at intervals
throughout the morning, each broadside agitating the breasts
of the accused with the belief that the final reckoning had
arrived and they would now, at last, know their fate. A mass of
people gathered, eager to discover, and to watch, the form of
punishment the queen had devised for the miscreants. But the
awful suspense was maintained until mid-morning:

*And then, accompanied by their escort, and marching to the
sound of military music, with all the solemn pomp belonging
to their rank and duties, the officers and judges, with their
attendants, arrived, and delivered the message of the Queen,
which was as follows:*

*I, Ranavalona Manjaka, Queen of Madagascar, say that no
religion whatever, excepting that of Andrianampoinimerina and
Radama, and the customs of your ancestors, shall be ever
introduced and practised in this my country; anything else is
totally rejected by me. Had I not ordered the followers of the new
religion to inculpate themselves, they would soon overturn the
country, and all the people would follow them. I consider them
rebels; therefore I tell you how I have punished them, as the
spirits of Andrianampoinimerina and Radama have revealed to me.*

The sentences on the 'rebels' were then read out. Over 1,800
of the prisoners, accused of merely taking part in Christian

worship, were fined according to their status: the poorest forfeiting three oxen and three dollars in quittance of their crime, while high officers of the palace were deprived of all rank and fined fifty dollars. Prince Ramonja was fined one hundred dollars and in an additional humiliation – to the consternation of many who believed him inviolate because of his royal blood – was reduced from his officer status to the rank of common soldier.

The severity of the sentences increased. Of the remaining 135 prisoners, 117 were sentenced to labour for life in chains (with 105 of these unfortunates to be flogged also). The final eighteen, including four Christian nobles, were marked for death: the fourteen commoners by being hurled from Ampamarinana, the Malagasy Tarpeian Rock, while their wives and children were to be sold into perpetual slavery. In consideration of the taboo against shedding royal blood, the four nobles were ordered burned alive at Favarohita, the last village on the northern end of the mountain on which the capital itself was built. The four included a husband and wife, the latter heavily pregnant. They requested, as a kindness, that they might be strangled just prior to the sentence of burning being carried out, but even this small mercy was peremptorily refused.

Those fourteen condemned to die at Ampamarinana had already been stripped naked and 'wrapped in torn and soiled pieces of matting in token of their degradation, their mouths filled with rag to prevent their speaking'. Now each was bound with cords to two rough poles and carried by bearers, trussed like trophy animals of a successful hunt, along the paths, lined with spectators, that led to Ampamarinana. As a concession to her kinship to the royal family and her former role as queen's favourite, 'the young and faithful Ranivo' alone was spared this indignity, and was left to walk apart at the end of the illustrious line to the place of execution:

*Here, on top of a lofty precipice, at the edge of the western crest of the mountain on which the city is built, the matting wrapped around their bodies was removed, but their arms remained pinioned, and their ankles were bound with cords. Thus bound they were taken, one by one, to the edge of the precipice, and either pushed, or laid down and rolled, or kicked over the downward curving edge. (MartyrChurch)*

But they did not die immediately; yet another, final trial was placed before the martyrs. According to another informant, their fall was suddenly arrested after some five or six feet by a rope

*firmly tied around the body of each ... While in this position, and when it was hoped by their persecutors that their courage would fail, the executioner, holding a knife in his hand, stood waiting for the command of the officer to cut the rope. Then, for the last time, the question was addressed to them, 'Will you cease to pray?' But the only answer returned was the emphatic 'No'.*

On this, the signal was given, the executioner's knife sliced through the cords of the rope, and

*they fell fifty or sixty feet, when, striking a projecting ledge, they bounded off and fell among jagged and broken fragments of granite lying at the base of the precipice, one hundred and fifty feet below the edge from which they had been hurled. Life was generally extinct.*

On the orders of the queen, who still harboured the desire to save her kinswoman, Ranivo was forced to watch the flight of her thirteen compatriots to this bloody death, before her own turn came. She

*was then led by the executioner to the edge of the rock and ordered to look down upon the mangled bodies of her friends. Her relatives entreated her to take the oath [to worship the idols], save her own life, and please her sovereign. But she begged that she might follow her friends, as she would not take the oath.*

The executioner then seized her. But instead of casting her immediately from the rock, he dragged her back from the edge, and contented himself with merely slapping her in the face, declaring 'she is insane, take her to her parents'. There is no doubt that this was done directly under the orders of Ranavalona; it seems that she retained a true affection for the young girl and, even while commanding that her former favourite be tested quite literally to the brink of death, she could not bring herself to order her demise. (Ranivo was finally sent to a village deep in the countryside, some thirty miles from the capital, and held under strong guard. She lived a long life, eventually marrying a Christian convert, and later raised two or three children in the foreign faith.)

If there was compassion of a kind for Ranivo, for the four condemned nobles Ranavalona showed not a scintilla of pity. By this time they had been carried from the plain to Faravohitra, located on the highest part of the hill. As a concession to their rank, none of the four had been gagged and they had spent what little time remained to them in singing the hymn *Hod izahay Zanahary*, 'Going home to God', crying out the last verse, which included the words

> *When we shall die*
> *And depart from this earth*
> *Then increase our joy;*
> *Take us to Heaven,*
> *Then rejoice*
> *Shall we forever more.*

At Faravohitra a huge pile of brushwood and kindling had been prepared, and the four were immediately fastened to stakes a little above the woodpile, the husband and his heavily pregnant wife bound side by side. As torches were applied the condemned were heard to ask forgiveness on their executioners' behalf: 'Lord Jesus receive our spirits – lay not this sin to their charge.' And strangely, the heavens seemed to respond, for a sudden downpour drenched the scene, extinguishing the hungry flames.

Given the Malagasy (and especially the queen's) penchant for superstition, it is surprising that this was not regarded as some extraordinary omen requiring special consideration, and the *auto da fe* halted, at least temporarily. But the executioners ignored the storm and went doggedly about their work, rekindling the flames until the whole woodpile was burning strongly. At this moment of horror, as the fire began its baleful work, a triple rainbow (seemingly the result of the passing storm) was said to have burst across the sky above the place of execution. This second 'sign' proved too much for many of the crowd, who fled the scene filled with supernatural terror. Those who remained witnessed the final horror of the execution: the stress and pain of the fire brought on the pangs of labour and, as the blaze took her own life, the pregnant noblewoman gave birth – only to see her newborn infant mercilessly thrown back into the flames.

These pitiless repressions of the foreign faith proved singularly counterproductive. The executions did nothing to stem the tide of those accepting Christianity; rather, the continuing persecutions, and the converts' cheerful demeanour in the face of death, impressed some sections of the populace with the power of new creed's teachings. The anti-Christian faction had made much of '*vazah* lies', claiming that the converts were just as afraid to die as anyone else. And yet here were ordinary men and women singing as they were marched away to their certain destruction, and scorning the chance of escape if the price of life was apostasy. However, just as many found the converts' behaviour incomprehensible and chose to remain true to the old gods.

This religious dichotomy was reflected in the new political division that sprang up at court. Up until 1852 the queen's old lovers, the brothers Rainiharo and Rainijohary, had continued to hold their position as her chief ministers, with both men supporters of the traditionalist party. But Rainiharo had died that year and his post of commander-in-chief had been passed on to his eldest son, Raharo. Another of Rainiharo's sons, Rainilaiarivony, was then advanced to the position of 'thirteen honours' and promoted to private secretary of the queen. Both these young bloods had been educated in the missionary schools and were therefore far more inclined to European ideas of government, which made them natural allies of Prince Rakoto, the queen's son, whose time with Jean Laborde had likewise disposed him to foreign ways. The old guard (known contemptuously to the Europeans as the 'idol worshippers') continued to be led by Rainijohary, and it was common knowledge at court that the old man would support the pretensions of Prince Ramboasalama, cousin to Prince Rakoto (and elder brother of the 'Christian Prince' Ramonja), should the throne for any reason become vacant. Sides were already being taken for an eventual power struggle, a process that was to have tragic consequences for all concerned.

Such manoeuvrings placed the queen in an invidious position. There is no doubt that, despite her bloodthirsty disposition, she loved her son and had always planned that he would succeed her. But at the same time her loyalty to the fetish, the *sikidy* and the old ways remained unshakeable. It may be that she hoped to bring him to power, but surrounded by a powerful traditional 'government' that would hold his modernising tendencies in check. If so, the rise of a 'modernist' faction within the government following Rainiharo's death in 1852, together with the increasing prevalence of Christianity within the populace, and especially within the nobility, may well have given her an opportunity to moderate her anti-European stance. This readjustment of the political equilibrium appears to have been the main reason for the thawing of Euro-Malagasy relations that commenced towards at the middle of 1853.

# CHAPTER SIXTEEN

# Lambert and Laborde

On July 18, 1853 the schooner *Gregorio* hove to at Tamatave roadstead and the Reverend William Ellis, foreign secretary of the London Missionary Society, stepped ashore carrying a letter from the traders of Mauritius for the 'Great Queen of Madagascar, Ranavalona-Manjaka'. He was met by an officer who, sixteen years earlier, had been part of the Malagasy embassy to England in 1837. This officer, now captain of Tamatave port, while sympathetic to the Englishman's mission, informed Ellis in no uncertain terms that the queen still smarted under the 'insult' of the Franco-British attack on Tamatave, and that until reparation for that outrage was made, Her Majesty had made clear that neither trade nor negotiation would be permitted. Such was the depth of resentment felt by the queen that nothing less than the sum of fifteen thousand dollars could efface the insult. Only then would the queen once again shine her face upon the traders.

Ellis took this information back to Mauritius and the merchants did their calculations. They very quickly realised that the cost of the 'reparation' was a worthwhile investment – the profits to be made from the Madagascan trade would rapidly repay the small cost each would incur in raising the required sum. By October 10 that year the cash had been carried to Madagascar by the veteran artisan-cum-missionary James Cameron, and forwarded to the queen at Antananarivo. This was followed by an immediate lifting of the embargo, and goods began once again to flow between Madagascar and the French and British islands in the Indian Ocean.

To the European traders, the payment of this 'fine' was a simple business matter, unfortunate and expensive no doubt, yet a necessary expedient to ensure the reopening of trade. But for Ranavalona the symbolic nature of the act was immense. This was a huge diplomatic coup for the queen. She had refused to bow before the combined demands of two of the most powerful nations on Earth. More, she had outfaced them, and insisted on redress for the damage these nations had visited on her own state. Steadfast and resolute, she had held to her ground unblinking, despite their threats and blandishments and, incredibly, these proud and arrogant *vazah* had eventually capitulated, returning cap in hand with the required indemnity. It was unheard of. No doubt the British and French saw it differently, but for the Malagasy it was unconditional surrender. The payment of the 'fine', in full, raised Merina morale to new heights, stirred their pride, and consolidated Ranavalona's image in the nation's eyes as an all-wise, invincible monarch. It was, quite simply, her triumph.

At the same time, the queen gave permission to remove the heads (or rather, as they now were, skulls) of the European sailors and soldiers killed during the attack on Tamatave, which still hung from their posts along the shore. The Governor of Mauritius, Mr Higginson, sent men to procure the heads, but found on arrival that the remains had already been taken down by the French and buried at Ile Ste Marie.

As well as a resultant welcome influx of cash to the Great Red Island, the resumption of trade brought yet another French adventurer to Malagasy shores in the shape of Monsieur Joseph Lambert. Born at Redon in 1824, at the age of twenty-two he had married a widow of a wealthy Mauritius planter, which gave him access to one of the biggest fortunes on that island of wealthy men.

Not content with these riches, Lambert began trading in negroes between Mozambique and the French Island of Bourbon. As the slave trade was illegal (and strictly enforced by British warships), Lambert and others devised a system whereby the negroes were guaranteed their freedom after five years and, in addition to food and lodgings, were each paid the paltry sum of two ecus per month for their labour. The British government grudgingly tolerated the trade as being not quite slavery; Lambert grew even richer and turned his eyes south towards resource-rich Madagascar, where even greater fortunes might be made. Nor was he ignorant of the long-standing interest his own nation had in the eventual inclusion of the Great Red Island within the French sphere of influence. Lambert was rich, but he had no title. Were he able to help effect the annexation of Madagascar to France, who knows what honours might be heaped on him by a grateful French government?

Lambert's chance came in 1854, on one of his occasional visits to the Malagasy coast. Hearing that a Merina garrison at Fort Dauphin was under siege from local tribes, and on the point of surrender owing to near starvation, Lambert offered to use his ship to carry rice and other relief supplies to the beleaguered garrison. His proposal was accepted with alacrity, Lambert sailed immediately, and the garrison was saved. Queen Ranavalona was not ungrateful for the Frenchman's help, and as a reward for his aid granted him the right to travel to the Merina capital and a royal audience.

Many accounts, especially the French reports, portray Lambert as a simple trader, intent only on opening new markets for his expanding business empire; but a closer analysis of his actions reveals other motives. He was certainly an entrepreneur par excellence, but there is no doubt that he was, at the same time, playing a much deeper and longer game. For when he took up Ranavalona's invitation to visit Antananarivo some months later, he did not travel to the capital alone but brought with him a European secretary, a Monsieur Finaz, who was, in fact, a Jesuit missionary in disguise. Right from the start, Lambert's relationship with Ranavalona and the Merina people was to be based on deceit.

At the capital, the Frenchman's amiable personality, together with his open-handed dispensation of the lavish gifts he had brought, made him an immediate success with many of the nobles. He also made contact with his fellow countryman Jean Laborde, innocent enough behaviour for a Frenchman far from home, but at least one contemporary British commentator saw it as deeply suspect:

> *he was immediately initiated into the projects of Laborde and his coadjutors to overthrow the existing tyranny of the reigning monarch and to substitute a prince who would be a tool in the hands of the French.*

The English suspicions of a prearranged French plot may have been well founded. Although Lambert remained at the capital for just four weeks he seems to have achieved an inordinate amount in that short time. His main target was Prince Rakoto, the queen's heir and, as we have seen, possibly Laborde's son. Thanks to Laborde's permanent presence at the capital and his previous position as tutor to the young prince, Rakoto was already well enamoured of all things French, and Lambert was soon regarded by the heir as a trusted friend and confidant. So much so, that when Lambert left the capital a month after his arrival, he took with him a charter, signed by the prince, which allowed for the establishment of a French company in Madagascar, and granted monopoly rights in timber, mining and agriculture over most of Merina territory. However, these concessions had been granted by the crown prince only, not by the ruling monarch; they were in reality illegal. And they could be implemented only on the effective dethronement of his mother, Ranavalona-Manjaka. This alone must have been a powerful temptation to the French entrepreneur. If Prince Rakoto were ever fortunate enough to succeed to the throne of Imerina, Joseph Lambert would be due riches beyond even his ambitious imaginings.

Just as important to this scheme, Lambert (with Jean Laborde's help) had contrived to extract from Rakoto an even greater prize – a letter, signed by the prince and addressed to His Imperial Majesty the French Emperor Napoleon III, which requested the establishment of a French protectorate and if necessary an armed force to effect the removal of his mother from the throne. A second letter, 'not less explicit and formal from the principal Malagasy chiefs', had likewise been procured that reiterated the prince's request for French 'protection'.

These letters are themselves extremely suspicious in their timing. It seems inconceivable that Lambert, an absolute new-comer to Merina society, could have prevailed on both Prince Rakoto and many of the nobility to commit what was in effect a blatant act of treason – a crime that, if discovered, would carry with it the most terrible retribution – and to sign their names to documents that provided incontrovertible evidence of their per-fidious actions. Why should they do this, risk death and horrific suffering, on the basis of an acquaintance of no more than four weeks? It is hard to escape the conclusion that here we are in the presence of a conspiracy, long conceived and carefully planned; that Lambert's arrival was merely the final piece in a jigsaw that Jean Laborde had already painstakingly constructed during his lengthy stay at the capital, a long premeditated plot to oust the queen and bring Madagascar, finally, under French control.

Lambert now undertook to carry the incriminating letters to Europe, where they could be used to canvass support for military intervention by France, under the pretext of a coup headed by Prince Rakoto and leading members of the aristocracy.

If, indeed, the prince and his nobles were ever party to, or even aware of, such a plot. When challenged by the British missionary

William Ellis that same year, the heir to the throne gave a very different account of the drawing up of these incriminating letters. In an appraisal Ellis prepared for the British Foreign Secretary Lord Clarendon, Ellis reported:

> I have also to inform your Lordship that the prince and some of the officers were exceedingly anxious about the result of M Lambert's voyage to Europe, and applied to me very soon after my arrival [August 26] for any information I might possess on the subject. The prince was greatly surprised and deeply affected on becoming acquainted with the representations that had been made by M Lambert. He said the papers taken away by that gentleman, so far as he had been made acquainted with their contents, were simply a statement of the grievances of the people ... He further stated that he did not prepare the letters or papers taken by Monsieur Lambert, and had no knowledge of the intention to prepare any papers of the kind until they were completed; that they were written in the French language, of which he does not understand half a dozen words, and were, he believes, drawn up by the priest [Père Finaz masquerading as Lambert's secretary, M Hervier] assisted by MM Laborde and Lambert; that when the papers were presented to him M Laborde translated verbally the pages containing a statement of the grievances of the people, and then said 'If you think this is true, add your name to it'.

So, according to Ellis, the heir to the throne was claiming that the letters Lambert had carried back to Europe were the result of an elaborate fraud, the true contents distorted, and the signatures on them extorted by the continual and unrelenting pressure of those the prince took to be his friends. Other accounts say that the prince was plied with so much alcohol during this meeting that he became intoxicated and was only dimly aware of the proceedings. Ellis gives additional details, supplied by another of those present, later in his report:

> the papers were signed, and a sort of oath not to divulge the secret extorted by the priest from the prince, at the close of a dinner

*party; and a degree of compulsion, little short of absolute force,*
*was used to secure his signature; and that they held his hand on*
*the bible while the priest pronounced the oath.*

All this, of course, was unknown at the time of Lambert's European visit. As far as anyone was concerned, the Frenchman carried with him a genuine plea from the Crown Prince of Madagascar, a request for help to free him, and his long-suffering people, from the intolerable yoke of an autocratic tyrant. And he came within a whisker of achieving his goal.

In Paris, Lambert found a ready ear for his plans among many members of the French government. According to one account, the administration was 'unanimously in favour of an armed expedition against Madagascar', and the project would certainly have gone forward but for one lone objector to the scheme, who pointed out that France was already deeply embroiled in a costly war, against Russia in the Crimea, and that troops were in very short supply. In addition, it would not do to offend the British, presently allied to the French against Russia, with such a reckless adventure. Ordinarily, a single dissenter's comments would have carried very little weight against the combined mass of officials, but on this occasion the lone voice was that of Napoleon III, the emperor himself. And his opinion could not be ignored by any minister desirous of obtaining high office. So the government changed its stance, and agreed that any onslaught on Ranavalona and her regime must be a combined operation with the explicit consent of France's respected ally, Great Britain.

Lambert was sent off to London in the hope of persuading the British government to acquiesce to the joint annexation of the Great Red Island. But Her Britannic Majesty's men felt themselves far too thinly spread for yet another foreign venture – like the

French they were heavily committed in the Crimea, and the problems they faced in India (where the Indian 'mutiny' was to erupt less than a year later) made them extremely chary of further expansionist talk. Lambert was received cordially, but obtained little in the way of encouragement from the Foreign Secretary Lord Clarendon, who expressed only his vague interest in the formation of a joint Franco-British company to take advantage of the (illegal) concessions granted Lambert by Prince Rakoto. But he promised nothing else in the way of men, guns or money. Nor was there any acknowledgement, tacit or otherwise, that Britain would look the other way if the French moved unilaterally. The British knew of Napoleon III's misgivings, and were not minded to give their present ally any potential future advantage in the Indian Ocean. There is little doubt that, had the two countries combined in the project, it would have succeeded – Ranavalona had escaped deposition and humiliation by a hair's breadth. She owed her continued rule, solely and unknowingly, to the power of Napoleon III's veto.

In all this Ranavalona seemed to have played very little part. Not that she was unaware of the machinations of Joseph Lambert (or of her erstwhile lover Jean Laborde) – her network of spies was extensive and reached to all levels of Merina society – but it seems that she did not yet feel that the time was ripe to bring matters to a head. Perhaps she still believed that Laborde and his industrial complex were too valuable to risk. After all, any plot against her rule was still in the very earliest stages. If it failed, she could continue to maintain friendly relations with Laborde and his French compatriots (while keeping them, perhaps, on a slightly tighter leash than hitherto) and persist in the building of her arsenal and army in expectation of later conflicts. There was no doubt that, without Laborde, her whole commissariat would fall into disarray, so it may simply have been prudent good sense to ignore the plotters and their schemes, until she discovered if their plans had thrived.

In addition, there was her son to consider. Even her most voracious critics are in accord with regard to the queen's deep feelings for the crown prince, and her desire that he should eventually rule in her stead. There was very little she would not do for him, and he was able on numerous occasions to use his mother's indulgence to mitigate the worst excesses of her rule, capping exorbitant taxes, preventing pogroms against Christians and dissuading her from condemning miscreants to horrific tortures. If Ranavalona were to publicly charge the plotters, the prince's part in the treason, unwittingly or otherwise, might also become common knowledge, greatly damaging his prestige and, indeed, that of the monarchy as a whole.

It was perhaps a wise strategy; for almost as soon as Lambert had left the Great Red Island rumours arose that he intended to return with a French army to annexe the kingdom. Even these vague whisperings served to strengthen the hand of Rainijohary, who was the leader of the more xenophobic wing of Merina society, and a supporter of the rival heir to the throne, Rambosalama.

Joseph Lambert's scheme to use the resources of the French and British governments was now in a shambles, but he was not a man to be easily thwarted. Guns and men might have been denied him, but he could still see a way by which his plans might succeed, using weapons with which he was much more familiar – the power of money and the greed of gain. He set the fiasco of his meeting with Lord Clarendon behind him and returned quickly to Paris, where he used his extensive connections and undoubted charm to win over a number of wealthy French businessmen to his cause. His new company, the Compagnie de Madagascar, Foncierre, Industrielle et Commerciale, possessed, on paper at least, monopoly rights to all the mines, timber and agricultural land of the Great Red Island, and there was no shortage of investors willing to advance Lambert enormous sums of money in the hopes of securing a slice of this lucrative venture. Such wealth would grease many Malagasy palms and would, he was certain, ensure the success of the coup he planned against the queen.

In Paris Lambert spent wildly, devoting over 200,000 francs of the investors' cash to the purchase of richly brocaded uniforms for

Prince Rakoto and his nobles. At the same time he bought up a gallimaufry of curiosities and exotica, barrel organs, musical clocks and similar toys, with which he believed he could allay the suspicions of Ranavalona and delight her ladies. Nor did he neglect the possibility of failure: a vessel was hired and commanded to Dalrymple Bay (Bavotoby), to act as a means of escape should the coup fail and flight prove inevitable.

With everything in readiness, Lambert began his return to Madagascar, stopping en route at his wife's home island of Mauritius. It was on the British island that, by chance, he was to meet and ensnare in this complex web of intrigue an extra-ordinary woman whose only real crime was an inordinate and sometimes reckless love of adventure and travel. She was a female traveller greatly celebrated in her own time but now, sadly, for the most part forgotten – the Austrian explorer, Madame Ida Pfeiffer.

# CHAPTER SEVENTEEN

# `A Strong Desire to See the World´

At that time, Ida Pfeiffer was probably the most celebrated woman traveller of her age. In a period renowned for its subjugation of women, with its insistence on regarding the 'weaker sex' as fragile flowers who would wilt at the first sign of hardship or sight of blood, Ida had travelled alone to more remote parts of the globe than most of the more famous male Victorian explorers.

She had begun her life as Ida Reyer, born in 1797 in Vienna, the only girl in a family of five or six brothers. Her father seems to have been something of an iconoclast – against the social mores of the time, he treated his only daughter just like her brothers, giving her the same educational advantages, encouraging her to play the same rough-and-tumble games, and even allowing her to wear boys' clothing most of the time. Unfortunately, when she was just nine years old her father died, and Madame Reyer (who seems to have regarded her husband's progressive principles with barely suppressed disapproval) immediately put in place a timetable of activities 'more suitable for a young lady of her time'. Ida was persuaded to wear feminine attire and take up piano lessons.

Like most well-brought-up ladies of her class, she was eventually provided with a tutor – and promptly fell in love with him. Her feelings were reciprocated and with all the naïve optimism of a seventeen year old, she confidently expected to marry her beloved. But once again Mama stepped in to thwart her happiness. She demanded a much better match for her daughter and refused to agree to the union. Ida was eventually married off at the age of twenty-two to a man much older than herself, Herr Pfeiffer, a lawyer with an important position in the Austrian government. Though it was scarcely an ideal love match, the union resulted in two sons.

Shortly after that, her husband lost his prestigious government position and the family fell on hard times, with Ida forced to give art and piano lessons in an attempt to make ends meet. Her mother's death in 1831 brought a small inheritance that was used to fund the boys' education, but tensions between Ida and her husband increased and four years later the couple separated. She continued to provide for her children, but by 1842 both of her sons had set up their own homes and Ida was finally liberated from the day-to-day cares of family life. She was also free of any obligation to her estranged husband. She decided, at the age of forty-five, to devote the rest of her life to travel. She wrote later:

> When I was but a little child, I had already a strong desire to see the world. Whenever I met a travelling carriage, I would stop involuntarily, and gaze after it until it disappeared.

Given the zeitgeist of her time, it was an extraordinary decision, the more so as the vast majority of travellers were men and of independent income, whereas she, a 'defenceless' woman, was all but penniless. Her family and friends were horrified and regarded her ambition as little short of suicide. Nevertheless, the confidence and self-reliance of her father's early teaching seem to have instilled in her an unshakeable belief in her ability to perform whatever she had set her mind to.

Rather cannily, she chose as her first adventure a 'pilgrimage' to the Holy Land, sure in the knowledge that the apparent religious aspect of her journey would do much to allay any fears, and disarm the worst criticism that her plans might provoke. The trip took ten months, with Ida travelling down the Danube river to the Black Sea and thence to Constantinople. She travelled on to Jerusalem and then to Egypt, where she visited Cairo, the Pyramids and the Sphinx (and where she also tried camel riding), before returning home via Italy. She published her diary of the journey in 1846 as *Visit to the Holy Land, Egypt and Italy* and enjoyed a moderate success. More importantly, the funds generated by the book's publication could finance further travels.

But only just. Throughout her life, Ida's ambitions were always far in advance of the size of her purse. Fortunately, she possessed a very practical turn of mind, and soon worked out the most efficient (and low-cost) methods of journeying in the more remote and less salubrious corners of the world. She became, in effect, the world's first 'independent traveller', eschewing 'package tours' and setting out alone to whatever destination took her fancy. Her wanderings gave her experience of all modes of transport from camel to donkey and from canoe to schooner, and her journals are full of sound utilitarian information on surviving in 'heathen' climes. Her guidance for sea travel in her book *A Woman's Journey Round the World* includes the following commonsense advice on the type of diet the traveller can expect on board ship:

> *The following form the ordinary diet: tea and coffee without milk, bacon and junk, soup made with pease or cabbage, potatoes, hard dumplings, salted cod, and ship-biscuit. On rare occasions, ham, eggs, fish, pancakes, or even skinny fowls, are served out. It is very seldom, in small ships, that bread can be procured.*
>
> *To render the living more palatable, especially on a long voyage, passengers would do well to take with them a few additions to the ship's fare. The most suitable are: portable soup and captain's biscuit – both of which should be kept in tin*

*canisters to preserve them from mouldiness and insects – a good quantity of eggs, which, when the vessel is bound for a southern climate, should first be dipped in strong lime-water or packed in coal-dust; rice, potatoes, sugar, butter, and all the ingredients for making sangaree and potato-salad, the former being very strengthening and the latter very cooling. I would strongly recommend those who have children with them to take a goat as well.*

A trip to Scandanavia and Iceland followed, which she wrote up as *Journey to Iceland, and Travels in Sweden and Norway*. Funds from this (together with rock and plant samples she had enterprisingly collected in Iceland and subsequently sold to various museums) allowed her to contemplate her most ambitious project yet – an odyssey around the world. In 1846 – just as Ranavalona had stirred up a hornet's nest by embargoing all trade between her realm and the islands of Mauritius and Reunion – Ida began her newest adventure, sailing for Brazil in the 'Caroline', a Danish brig and arriving at Rio de Janeiro on 16$^{th}$ September, after a voyage of just over six weeks. Most travel writers of the time had praised the city for its superb scenic location, but true to her iconoclastic style, Ida berated Rio's urban squalor and poverty, before setting out with a guide into the rain forest in search of a tribe of Puri Indians. Her description of that journey reveals that she found the rain-forest environment enchanting and exciting by turns. But once again, humanity disappointed – like many European ladies of her day, Ida had a well-developed sense of her own Christian/European superiority, and when faced with other cultures there was little she could find in them to commend. The Puri were, she thought, both primitive and savage.

After South America she travelled to the orient via Tahiti (where she was both disgusted and outraged by the sexual freedom of the native women), sailing first to the Portuguese colony of Macao on the southern coast of the Chinese empire. Travelling by junk, a traditional Chinese cargo boat, she sailed alone to the capital city of southern China, the sprawling, bustling city of Guangdong (Canton), where she visited Louis Agassiz, the well-known biologist, who was studying there. But Ida was not one to stay in the relative safety of the European sphere of influence in the city, and despite the most dire warnings of her new acquaintances she made many excursions around Guangdong, though she took her friends' advice and disguised herself as a man for safety. As with her observations of South America, she took a rather superior attitude to the ancient culture of China, and her opinion of the locals and their customs was almost uniformly negative:

> *The Chinese are cowardly in the highest degree; they talk very large when they are certain they have nothing to fear. For instance, they are always ready to stone, or even kill, a few defenceless individuals, but if they have to fear any opposition, they are sure not to commence the attack ... I myself never met with a more dastardly, false, and at the same time, cruel race, in my life.*

Chinese justice seemed to her extreme:

> *the more severe punishments, which in no way yield the palm to the Holy Inquisition, consist in flaying the prisoner alive, crushing his limbs, cutting the sinews out of his feet, and so on. Their modes of carrying out the death sentence appear mild in comparison, and are generally confined to strangling and decapitation, although, I was informed, in certain extraordinary cases, the prisoner is executed by being sawn in two ... the unhappy victim is made fast between two planks, and sawed in two longitudinally, beginning with the head.*

She was especially shocked by the stories of infanticide, with the Chinese accused of killing both weakling and female babies.

> *They are said to suffocate them immediately after birth, and then throw them into the river, or expose them in the streets – by far the most horrible proceeding of the two, on account of the number of swine and houseless dogs, who fall upon and voraciously devour, their prey.*

Ida's next port of call, India, was much more to her liking, and she spent several months there, travelling with almost no baggage. Almost incredibly, given the age in which she lived, she travelled through the country alone, carrying only a leather pouch for water, salt, bread and rice, and a small pan for cooking. She was often hungry, but her unusual appearance and behaviour gave her much of the kudos of a wandering native sadhu and she was fed and given shelter by the local people. Leaving the Indian subcontinent, she continued her journey by land, travelling unscathed through the wild tribal regions and eventually reaching Baghdad in Mesopotamia (now known as Iraq). Here, still completely alone, she joined a camel caravan and undertook a 300-mile odyssey north-west across the desert sands to the city of Mosul in Kurdistan, before striking out north-east to ancient Tabriz in northern Persia (now Iran). The British consul stationed in Tabriz was astonished to hear that a lone white woman had arrived in the city from India, and at first refused to believe the story. When Ida eventually turned up at the consulate he confessed that he simply did not think it possible for a woman to travel alone in that part of the world, without even knowing the local languages.

By this time Ida was tired of journeying through countries she considered backward – civilisation beckoned and she was happy to follow. When she discovered that a caravan was leaving Tabriz for the Russian border, she joined it eagerly. She was, she admitted, looking forward to seeing Christian folk again. They, unfortunately, were not quite as happy to see her. She was soon arrested by the Tsar's secret police, and held overnight under suspicion of being a spy, while her identity was confirmed. Ida found her treatment intolerable, especially from fellow Christians, and looked back kindly on her time among the so-called heathen, writing in her journal:

*Oh you good Arabs, Turks, Persians, Hindoos! How safely did I pass through your heathen and infidel countries; and here, in Christian Russia, how much have I had to suffer in this short space.*

She was, however, eventually accepted as a simple, though by no means usual, traveller and allowed to go on her way. Continuing westwards, she journeyed through Turkey, Greece and Italy and eventually returned home in November 1848, two years after her travels had begun. She quickly published an account of her adventures under the title *A Woman's Journey Around the World*. The book was a sensation, and established Ida as one of the great travellers of any age.

All this might well have satisfied the wanderlust and taste for adventure of any ordinary traveller, man or woman. But Ida's restless spirit would not leave her long in idleness, and in 1851 she undertook a second world tour, travelling eastwards via London and Cape Town to the islands of Indonesia, where she braved the forests of Borneo, Sumatra and the Celebes (now Sulawesi), eschewing European company and spending as much time as possible with the local inhabitants, eating their food and observing such strange ceremonies as the Celebean tooth-filing festival.

Given her avowed dislike and oft-expressed contempt for 'primitive' peoples, Ida's time with the headhunting Dyaks in Borneo was a revelation, for she found in their culture many admirable qualities. Perhaps she was mellowing, for her journal contains the following:

> *I shuddered, but I could not help asking myself whether, after all, we Europeans are not really just as bad or worse than these despised savages? Is not every page of our history filled with horrid deeds of treachery and murder? ... I should like to have passed a longer time among the free Dyaks, as I found them, without exception, honest, good-natured, and modest in their behaviour. I should be inclined to place them, in these respects, above any of the races I have ever known.*

Such approbation did not extend to the next tribe she visited, the cannibal Batak of Sumatra in the Dutch East Indies. Although warned that her journey would end in disaster (up until then the Batak had refused to allow Europeans to enter their territory, and as recently as 1855 they had killed and eaten three French missionaries who had dared to trespass), this redoubtable middle-aged matron pressed on with her plans and spent several weeks as the Batak's guest. She persuaded them to show her their rituals, and even to mimic the sacred dance that preceded the eating of a captive. Using a log in place of a man, and substituting a straw cap for the head,

> *the dancers lifted up their feet as high as they could and darted their knives in the most expressive manner. At length one of them gave the first stroke – they struck the head (the straw cap, namely) from the body, and laid it upon a mat spread out to receive it, taking care to preserve the blood. They then danced around it, uttering wild and joyful cries. Some raised the head in their hands and carried it to their lips, appearing to lick the blood from it; others flung themselves on the ground and appeared to be lapping up the gore from the dripping head, or they dipped their fingers into it and sucked them; doing all this with the appearance of the greatest delight ... I could not witness it without some shuddering, especially when I considered that I was entirely in the power of these wild cannibals.*

For their part, the Batak appear to have treated Ida as a curiosity, and passed her from tribe to tribe for inspection and entertainment. But the risk of death was never far away. On one occasion the tribesmen indicated that they wished to kill and make a meal of her, but she disarmed their threat by passing it off as a joke, describing in the little Batak she had learned how old and stringy she was, and what tough eating she would make. The tribesmen found her response amusing and made no move against her, but from that time on she never felt safe in their presence. Eventually, she found an opportunity to escape, and returned safely to Batavia (now Jakarta) with the first eyewitness account of Batak culture.

From the Indonesian archipelago Ida then sailed for the relative comfort and safety of San Francisco, later voyaging down the west coast to Lima in Peru, from whence she visited Ecuador and journeyed high into the Andes Mountains. Four years after she had set out she finally returned home, and immediately penned *A Woman's Second Journey Around the World*, which became an almost instant bestseller in most European languages. Because of her pioneering work in the fields of exploration and anthropology, Ida Pfeiffer was elected as a member of the geographical societies of both Paris and Berlin. To its everlasting shame, the Royal Geographical Society in Britain, while acknowledging her achievements, refused her admittance solely on the grounds of her sex.

At the age of sixty, when most ladies of her time were contemplating quiet retirement and a genteel old age, Ida Pfeiffer decided on yet another trip, this time to the fabled isle of Madagascar. Permission to travel in the interior of Madagascar was difficult to obtain, but she decided, as a first step, to travel via South Africa to Mauritius, and to see from there how the land lay. Given her earlier travels and the many dangers she had successfully survived, the journey to Mauritius can hardly have given her much pause for thought. Yet this simple trip was to be her undoing.

Ida began her latest expedition on May 21, 1856, sailing to the Cape of Good Hope and thence to Mauritius. Here, while she awaited an opportunity to obtain passage to Tamatave (and hopefully to gain permission to visit the capital), she busied herself visiting the island's sugar-cane plantations and beauty spots, including the famous Trou de Cerf, 'a crater of perfectly regular formation, brimful of bloom and foliage'.

It was Ida's misfortune to arrive on the island of Mauritius at the very time that Joseph Lambert had returned from his abortive trip to Europe, loaded with gifts and geegaws with which he hoped successfully to foment the revolution that would remove Ranavalona, place Prince Rakoto on the throne, and give effective control of the island to France – and (perhaps his most important consideration) make him both fabulously wealthy and an aristocrat to boot. On such a small island it was inevitable that the famous Austrian traveller and the flamboyant French adventurer should meet. When he learned of Ida's desire to visit the Madagascan capital and see the notorious Female Caligula at first hand, Lambert offered to use his influence at the Malagasy court to escort her to Antananarivo, which was, by happy circumstance, the goal of his own journey.

The British governor of Mauritius knew of Lambert's revolutionary scheming, and tried to warn his Austrian guest of the dangers she faced in associating herself with the Frenchman. The same fears had been echoed by Mr McLeod, the English consul at Mozambique. He, too, had become apprised of Lambert's plot and of the escape boat anchored at Dalrymple Bay, and begged Ida to reconsider.

But all such warnings were in vain. Perhaps, having escaped so many dangers in so many remote locations, Ida Pfeiffer had come to believe in her own legendary status and to deem herself invulnerable to all perils. Possibly she approved of the coup and wished to be in at the kill when the revolution was successfully accomplished. It would, after all, have been a fitting climax to the new book she planned on the wonders of the Great Red Island. To be the first to report the revolution, the demise of the notorious Ranavalona and the arrival of a Christian government would have been a literary coup of gigantic proportions and would have all but guaranteed the success of any publication. Or maybe it was Ida's elemental love of adventure that prevailed over all her fears. The possibility of being one of the very few Europeans to visit Antananarivo, the forbidden capital of the Merina, and to see at first hand the atrocious African Queen was perhaps too much of a temptation for Ida, and she simply chose to turn a blind eye to the obvious dangers.

To the general disapproval of the British authorities, when the sloop *Triton* left Mauritius on April 25, 1857 and set its prow towards Madagascar, Ida Pfeiffer was on board, determined to travel with Joseph Lambert to this strange land and to view the Sanguinary Queen in her own capital.

# CHAPTER EIGHTEEN

# Journey to the Sanguinary Queen

The passage was stormy and it took six days to complete the voyage of 480 sea miles (890 kilometres) from Mauritius to Madagascar. True to form, when she did finally arrive at the port of Tamatave on May 1, 1857, Ida Pfeiffer was disappointed. Tamatave, the most important roadstead of the Merina kingdom, home to four or five thousand souls, was not the major entrepot she expected; she found it crammed and dirty and thought it resembled nothing so much as 'a poor but very large village'. Lambert had not yet arrived on the island and she was forced to take up residence in the port, at a hotel of sorts, presided over by its obese mistress, 'Mademoiselle Julie'. Ida was shocked to find this particular 'mademoiselle' to be of middle age and with several children to her credit, for

> in Madagascar, the strange custome prevails of calling every member of the sex feminine 'madamoiselle' even though she may have a dozen little olive branches to show, or may have been married half a dozen times.

Lambert did not appear for several weeks, which gave Ida ample opportunity to observe Malagasy custom in the person of Mlle Julie. She found little to praise:

> *Her greatest delight is to lie for hours extended on the ground, resting her head on the lap of a friend or female slave, who is engaged in clearing Madamoiselle's head of certain little occupants which shall be nameless. This agreeable occupation, by the way, forms a diversion of the women, who pay visits to each other in order to indulge in it* con amore. *Madame Julie was also violently addicted to using her fingers at dinner, instead of fork and spoon.*

Nor was Ida taken with the Malagasy menu at the 'hotel', bemoaning the monotonous meals of rice and anana (a type of spinach) and the lack of fresh meat, which despite being cheap and in good supply was eaten only on special occasion. But Ida kept her greatest opprobrium for the ubiquitous beverage named *ranu-gang*, with which she was expected to wash down her rice and anana. To produce this delicacy, the Malagasy boiled rice in a stewpot until it was burned to a cinder and a dark black crust had formed at the bottom of the pan. Then more water was added and the whole boiled again to produce a pale coffee liquid

> *in taste abominable to a European palate. The natives, however, esteem it greatly and not only drink the water, but eat the crust.*

It was more than a month before Joseph Lambert finally put in an appearance at Tamatave, but once arrived, he lost no time in organising the expedition to Antananarivo. The first three days of any journey to the Merina capital was by canoe, via the lagoons or *pangalanes* that lay behind the enormous ranks of sand dunes along the coast. The going was easy here, with short portages between the lakes a welcome break from the monotonous dip of the paddles on the mirror-calm waters. This leg of the journey ended at Andevoranto, where a foot trail turned towards the island's interior. Lacking roads, the traveller normally journeyed on foot, but for Ida and her companion *filanjana* were provided.

These were primitive sedan chairs, no more than a seat slung on two long bamboo poles, and carried by four men, with four more in reserve. As the first quartet of bearers tired, the remaining four were practised enough to take over the weight of the chair and passenger without even breaking stride. Over good ground the *filanjana* could maintain speeds of around ten kilometres per hour, throughout the day.

From Andevoranto the trail rose steadily into the hills of the interior, passing bamboo-clothed valleys and rushing torrents, hard enough to travel in the dry season but almost impassable during wet weather. Each night they would find rest at one of the larger villages on the path, which served as posthouses for travellers to and from the capital. By the sixth day they had reached Taninkova, 'the weeping place of the Hova', where slaves making the reverse journey from capital to coast saw their first view of the sea that was to carry them far from home and family.

From here the trail became more precipitous, as they moved from the secondary growth of the foothills onto the first escarpment of the interior clothed with tall, virgin forest. Beyond, on a narrow belt of tableland, lay Lake Alaotra, the island's largest stretch of fresh water, and beyond this the steep trail of the second escarpment that gave out onto the high plateau, homeland of the Merina people. They had left the dark primary forest behind them now and travelled through rolling hills and paddy fields, dotted with prosperous villages, stopping for a final night's rest at Ambatomanga, from which they could see their destination, the capital Antananarivo, perched on its craggy height some 500 feet above the rest of the plateau.

It was custom for every visitor to wait for at least eight days in the capital before being granted an audience with the queen – if, indeed, they were ever fortunate enough to receive an invitation.

But just four days into their stay, on June 2, both Lambert and Ida were summoned to the royal presence, an almost unheard-of sign of favour from the Great Glory. Hurriedly dressing in their most formal clothes, they were carried in palanquins up the steep, narrow thoroughfares of the city to the palace. Set down at its entrance, they passed two great gates, the first surmounted by the statue of an enormous gilded eagle with outstretched wings, and Ida took great pains to cross the threshold of both gates with her right foot, as etiquette demanded. According to Merina tradition, it was death to enter the queen's domain with the left foot.

The second gate opened on to a great courtyard in front of the huge wooden chateau, and here Ida caught her first glimpse of the Sanguinary Queen, sitting enthroned on a balcony on the first floor. She was wrapped in a gorgeous Malagasy *simbu* of costly silk and wore a massive golden crown on her head. Attendants held above her the royal umbrella of scarlet silk, despite the fact that she was already sitting in deep shade. To the right of the throne stood her son, Prince Rakoto, and on the left his rival for the throne, Prince Rambosalama, the queen's adopted son and one-time heir, while behind the throne were a throng of royal nephews and nieces, together with sundry members of the nobility.

True to her fastidious character, Ida was less than impressed by the royal presence. She found Ranavalona

*of rather dark complexion, strong and sturdily built, and though already seventy-five years of age, she is, to the misfortune of her poor country, still hale and of active mind.*

She added the intriguing snippet that 'at one time she is said to have been a great drunkard, but she has given up that fatal propensity some time ago'.

The audience was very brief. A squadron of native soldiers, bravely dressed, stood just beneath the queen's balcony. They went through a drill sequence that, while no doubt intended to impress, Ida found surprisingly comical, especially when each concluded his set piece by suddenly and incongruously raising his right foot 'as if it had been stung by a tarantula'. A minister of the crown spoke a short speech of welcome to the visitors; they then bowed three times to the royal party, turned and bowed, again three times, to the tomb of the queen's husband King Radama, after which etiquette demanded that they return to their former position and perform a third triple bow in the queen's direction. Joseph Lambert then paid the requisite *monosina*, a gold piece of fifty francs value.

After the tribute had been received, the queen spoke for the first time, enquiring after Lambert's health and if he stood in need of any services. Ranavalona then turned her attention to her female guest and asked if she had managed to escape the fever that affected so many of the white people who visited her capital. Ida responded that she was quite well, and then an uncomfortable silence fell on the assembly, when for several minutes the queen simply stared at the two Europeans, saying nothing. Eventually they were dismissed and, after another set of obeisances to the balcony and to the tomb of the dead king, Ida and Lambert retired to their lodgings, being reminded once again as they departed of the fatal importance of crossing each threshold with their right foot.

Everything she had seen of Ranavalona on this first visit seemed to have prejudiced Ida even more against the native queen:

> She is certainly one of the proudest and cruel women on the face of the earth, and her whole history is a record of bloodshed and deeds of horror. At a moderate computation, it is reckoned that from twenty to thirty thousand people perish annually in Madagascar, some through the continual executions and poisonings, others through grievous labour purposely inflicted, and from warfare. If this woman's rule lasts much longer, the beautiful island will be quite depopulated, the population is said to have already shrunk to half the number it comprised in King Radama's time, and a vast number of villages have disappeared from the face of the land.

Ida's feelings for Prince Rakoto could not have been more different. She found the prince gentle, quiet and charming, and it appears that the heir to the throne was also very taken with the sexagenarian traveller and soon took her into his confidence. And here a story completely at odds with that brought back to England by the Reverend Ellis emerged, told to Ida Pfeiffer (or so she claimed) from the very mouth of the prince himself:

> At Antananarivo the prince himself told me the story of the signing of the treaty. He let me read the document, and assured me that the tale of the intoxication was a fiction; that he had perfectly understood what he was doing, and that he never repented this step at all.

There could now be no doubt at all as to Lambert and Laborde's intentions. The rumours of a coup that Ida had heard in Mauritius were replaced by the stone-cold certainty that Ranavalona's days as queen were numbered, that the crown prince was deeply implicated in the affair, that a coup d'état was imminent and that, through no fault of her own, Ida Pfeiffer was now considered a part of the conspiracy.

# CHAPTER NINETEEN

# Plots and Pianos

At that time Ida Pfeiffer was still completely ignorant of the components of the planned coup. All that changed on June 6, when Jean Laborde gave a sumptuous feast at his garden house, in honour of Prince Rakoto. Ida had been unwell with a Malagasy fever for several days previously, but was prevailed on to attend the banquet as an experience not to be missed.

Arriving by sedan chair around three o'clock in the afternoon, she found that an exhibition of native sports had been prepared for her by the considerate Frenchman, including an exhibition of foot boxing, in which the 'combatants kicked each other all over, and with such hearty goodwill, that I expected broken legs or ribs would be the result'. Several authorities have suggested that the sport may have been derived from *savate*, a French form of martial art, in which all four limbs are used in fencing with the opponent. If so, Jean Laborde made no mention of its provenance. Ida was told that the natives were particularly fond of the sport during the Malagasy winter, which stretched between May and July and saw temperatures dip to just above freezing on the high plateau. Only the rich could afford to bring firewood from the forest to heat their homes; and it seemed the remainder of the populace kept warm by alternately kicking each other.

Singers and dancers then took turns in entertaining the visitors, after which the guests were invited to tread a measure themselves. Between dances Joseph Lambert, no mean tenor, regaled the party with 'some very pretty songs'. Then, around ten in the evening, the whole timbre of the evening changed.

> Mr Laborde whispered to me that I should allege the weakness that still remained from my late indisposition, as a pretext for breaking up the party. I replied that this was not my province, but that of Prince Rakoto; but he urged me to do it, adding, that he had a particular reason for his request, which he would explain to me later; and accordingly I broke up the party.

By the light of a full moon, and led by a noisy group of musicians, the small party of Europeans, together with Prince Rakoto, then climbed the winding streets of the capital towards Lambert's dwelling house. Once inside, and secure from prying eyes, the prince and Lambert called Ida into a side room:

> where the prince declared to me once more that the private contract between himself and Mr Lambert had been drawn up with his full concurrence ... He told me further that Mr Lambert had come to Madagascar by his wish, and with the intention, in conjunction with himself and a portion of the nobility and soldiers, to remove Queen Ranavalona from the throne, but without depriving her of her freedom, her wealth, or the honours which were her due ... [Mr Lambert] then showed me in the house a complete little arsenal of sabres, daggers, pistols and guns, wherewith to arm the conspirators, and leather shirts of mail for resisting lance-thrusts; and told me, in conclusion, that all preparations had been made, and that the time for action had almost come – in fact, I might expect it every hour.

With this revelation, the true reality of the plot seems finally to have impinged itself on Ida's consciousness. Until that point it appears that, fired by her desire to see the removal of so terrible a despot, she had regarded the conspiracy in abstract, almost theoretical terms. But the sight of the weapons, those tangible instruments of death and mutilation, brought home to her the brutal fact of insurrection, and the terrible risk she had taken both in accompanying Joseph Lambert to the capital and in spending so much time in his company and that of his co-conspirators.

> *In a country like Madagascar, where everything depends on the despotic will of the ruler, no trouble is taken to determine the question of guilty or not guilty ... My friends in Mauritius had certainly warned me previously against undertaking the journey in Mr Lambert's company; and from what had been reported there, and likewise from some scattered words which Mr Lambert had let fall from time to time, I was able to form an idea of what was going on; but my wish to obtain a knowledge of Madagascar was so great that it stilled all fear. Now, indeed, there was no drawing back; and the best I could do was to put a good face upon a bad matter, and trust in that Providence which had already helped me in many and great dangers.*

Surrounded by the eager, smiling conspirators, her brain 'filled with a crowd of conflicting thoughts', Ida managed to wish the prince and Lambert great success in their venture, before pleading tiredness (it was now long past midnight) and retiring to her room. Here she was plagued throughout the night with restless thoughts and, when she did finally manage to fall into a fitful sleep, with an unsettling and perhaps premonitory dream.

She was standing with Lambert in a large room in the palace, summoned there by the queen. After what seemed an eternity of anguished waiting, Ranavalona and her court appeared, together with Prince Rakoto. But in the dream the prince moved aside to a window and pointedly ignored the two Europeans. Two ministers then spoke for the queen, the first haranguing Mr Lambert for his ingratitude and treachery, the second announcing the fate that Ida feared most – both prisoners were condemned to the *tanguena* ordeal.

*Hereupon we were led into another room, and a tall negro, wrapped in a full white garment, came towards us with the little skins of poison. Mr Lambert was obliged to take them first; but at the moment I was about to follow his example, there arose suddenly a loud din of music and rejoicing shouts, and – I awoke.*

The celebratory cacophany was no illusion. The origin of the joyous hubbub was the climax of a real *tanguena* ordeal that had taken place while she slept. Hurrying to the gate of her house, Ida discovered that two men had been condemned to the trial by poison that same night, but both had been able to vomit forth the poison and all three pieces of chicken skin and had therefore been declared guiltless of all crimes. Their friends, who if matters had turned out differently would be carrying two corpses for burial, now bore their 'innocent' compatriots back in triumph to their homes.

A singular coincidence: to dream of two condemned to the *tanguena*, and to awake and find two happily released from that same hellish ordeal. It was a conjunction of events whose seemingly prophetic nature can only have worked on the mind of the dreamer, if only subconsciously. But as is the nature of prophecies, this dream concealed far more than it revealed.

Helped by the bright light of day and the presence of her friends, Ida Pfeiffer's fears receded somewhat. On the surface all was pleasantry and goodwill between the queen and her European guests. Just three days after Ida's 'initiation' into the conspiracy, it was announced that the queen would hold a great fancy-dress ball at court, solely in honour of Mr Lambert. In her agitated state of mind, Ida remained sceptical and uneasy by this display of apparent royal favour. She asked in her journal:

*Does the Queen really doubt the existence of the treaty between Prince Rakoto and Mr Lambert? Or does she wish to let the conspirators commit some overt act, that she may afterwards satiate her revenge with apparent justice?*

There was simply no way of knowing. Ranavalona-Manjaka maintained her inscrutable distance, sitting in her grand wooden palace like a dark, malignant spider, quietly testing the many strings in her web of spies and informers, and capable at any moment of launching a fatal attack on the plotters.

The strain must have been intolerable, and yet all that Ida could do was to act as normally as possible, to go through the motions of a privileged guest in a strange land, while every day nobles and officers visited Lambert with an appalling disregard for even the most basic security: 'not a day passed in which greater or smaller kabars were not held in our house, which was, in fact, the headquarters of the conspiracy'.

The queen's ball began during the hottest part of the day, at one o'clock in the afternoon. It was not held in the palace, as Ida had expected, but outside in the vast forecourt where she had first been granted an audience with Her Majesty. Ranavalona remained aloof from the proceedings, enthroned on her balcony beneath the shade of the scarlet umbrella of state, watching the arrival of her guests, all of whom belonged to the higher aristocracy. Despite this, comfortable armchairs were provided only for the most honoured guests, the remainder of the exalted company being obliged to squat in their finery in groups on the dusty ground.

Almost all the guests wore European costume, as commanded by the queen. But as Ranavalona obtained most of her ideas of 'high fashion' from engravings or paintings that she chanced upon, the costumes had been elaborated on according to local taste with, as Ida pointed out with mischievous understatement, 'great boldness and originality in the combination of colours'. One of the female guests wore a dress

*of blue satin, with a border of orange colour above which ran a broad stripe of cherry-coloured satin. The body, also of satin, with long skirt, shone with a brimstone hue, and a light sea-green silk shawl was draped above it. The head was covered in such style with stiff, clumsily made artificial flowers, with ostrich feathers, silk ribbons, glass beads and all kinds of millinery, that the hair was entirely hidden – not that the fair one lost much thereby, but that I pitied her for the burden she had to carry ... The costumes of the other ladies showed similar contrasts in colour, and some of these tasteful dresses had been improved by a further stroke of ingenuity, being surmounted by high conical hats, very like those worn by the Tyrolese peasants.*

The men, by contrast, wore relatively sober dress, with French and Spanish costume predominating, mainly military uniform with an abundance of brocade and velvet, the cuffs and epaulettes swimming in silver and gold braid. Most of the nobles wore tricorn hats, with various plumes, which they removed while making the numerous obeisances to the queen that Malagasy etiquette demanded.

The entertainment began with the queen's dancers, all dressed alike in white *simbus*, performing a traditional measure that Ida, typically disdainful of Merina culture, described as 'the dreary Malagasy dance'. She was not much more impressed by the skills of the queen's officers, who while they danced 'set up a sharp howling, intended to represent cries of joy'. Next, there followed six pairs of children, the boys dressed in the Spanish style

*and looked tolerably well; but the girls were perfect scarecrows. They wore old-fashioned French costumes – large stiff petticoats with short bodices – and their heads were quite loaded with ostrich feathers, flowers and ribbons.*

But, much to her surprise, the children performed 'Polonaises, Schottisches and contre-danses' flawlessly, forcing this most demanding of European travellers to admit that they had acquitted themselves 'with considerable skill'. She was equally entranced by a performance of the *sega*, though she could not prevent herself from commenting that this dance was not, as the

Malagasy claimed, native to the country, but had in fact been borrowed from the Arab traders who frequented Madagascar's western shore.

A short pause followed this display, during which no refreshments whatever were offered to the guests. Then came the social climax of the ball, with another dancing display, this time by the elite of the company, Prince Rakoto, Jean Laborde, his son, two ministers and a general taking to the floor with female partners, each of whom was either a princess or a countess. While most of the men were dressed in old Spanish costume, Prince Rakoto

> wore a fancy dress so tastefully chosen, that he might have appeared with distinction in any European Court ball. He wore trousers of dark blue cloth, with a stripe down the side, a kind of loose jerkin of maroon-coloured velvet, ornamented with gold stripes and the most delicate embroidery, and a velvet cap of the same colour, with two ostrich feathers fastened by a golden brooch ... This group of dancers appeared with much more effect than their predecessors.

To Ida's obvious approval, 'they performed only European dances'.

The display proved to be the grand finale of the ball. The queen's court dancers closed the proceedings and, about three hours after it had begun, the revellers made their way to their separate homes. Ida's shrewd mind was quick to note that the festivities had cost the queen very little but her time:

> The courtyard was the dancing floor, the sun provided the illumination, and every guest was at liberty to take what refreshment he chose – when he got home. Happy queen! How sincerely many of our European ball-givers might envy her!

Three more days of terror and suspense followed this engaging interlude, in which Ida kept mainly to her bedroom, imagining an imminent arrest and starting at the bark of every dog or each new arrival at Lambert's house. In the meantime, the main actors in the plot took no action, spending their time in (to Ida) fruitless and interminable discussions, which in her opinion served only to increase the risk of discovery, for 'a traitor might easily be found among the nobles and officers apparently devoted to the prince'. She was also reappraising her estimation of the heir presumptive:

> *A good deal of the fault may lie with the prince himself. He is, as I have observed, a man of many good and noble qualities, but he wants decision and purpose; and his affection for the Queen is, moreover, so great, that he might lack courage at the decisive moment to undertake anything against her ... God strengthen him and give him courage to be the deliverer of his people!*

The prince had other weaknesses that may well have been hidden from Ida, but of which Laborde and Lambert cannot have been ignorant. While he undoubtedly possessed a humane and non-violent temperament most of the time, his apparently benevolent nature had its hidden dark side. From his early youth Rakoto had associated with a group of contemporaries known as the *menamaso* ('red eyes'). These young men were the heir's companions and, while they did much good work by helping Rakoto to protect Christians during his mother's persecution of the sect, they were also known for their wild ways. The *menamaso* arranged, and encouraged the prince to indulge in, what the missionary Ellis described as 'sinful habits' – the regular bouts of drunkenness and debauchery that were the traditional pastime of the male members of the royal clan. These orgies revealed a reckless and undisciplined side to Prince Rakoto's nature that worried his European friends and that, much later, was to give rise to the most disastrous consequences.

But before Prince Rakoto or any of the plotters could prove their mettle, there came the moment Ida had dreaded ever since she had been made aware of the conspiracy. Officers of

Ranavalona's court were drumming forcefully on the door of Lambert's house and demanding entry in the queen's name. They were allowed access immediately and, with her heart in her mouth, Ida went to meet them, expecting the proclamation of her imminent arrest, torture and no doubt grisly death.

Instead, she found herself invited to a piano recital – in which she herself was to star as chief pianist.

On his first visit to the Merina capital in 1853, Joseph Lambert had brought with him a profusion of presents for the queen, including a piano produced by Deboin of Paris. This instrument could not only be played in the normal manner, but was equipped with a *manivelle* or short handle that allowed it to be used as a barrel organ, producing a number of popular tunes. From one source or another (possibly from Lambert himself) the queen had learned that her foreign guest possessed some talent as a pianist, and had decided that she would see a performance immediately. There was only one problem:

*For more than thirty years I had given up music, and had nearly forgotten all I once knew. Who would ever have thought that I should have to give a concert, under royal patronage, in my sixtieth year ... But so it is when people go out in search of adventure, and roam through the wide world; one never knows what may happen, and must be prepared for everything.*

The invitation was, for Ida, a happy release from tension, a chance to forget the constant anxiety of the last weeks. And it would also give her the opportunity to view the inner chambers of the royal palace, of seeing the infamous Sanguinary Queen at close quarters in her lair. Lambert was indisposed with yet another bout of Madagascan fever, but nothing daunted, Ida asked the two French priests to accompany her to her recital. Unfortunately, Ranavalona had other ideas. When the trio arrived at the palace they were left outside in the main enclosure, watched silently by the queen 'on the eternal balcony ... It seemed I was to be treated like a street musician, and made to play here in the courtyard'.

But matters did improve slightly. Ida was invited indoors, and conducted by servants to the ground-floor gallery of the nearby silver palace, its doors and windows hung with innumerable silver bells, where the piano and several chairs awaited them. Ida had a brief glimpse of the interior, 'spacious and lofty and furnished quite in European style', but hung with paintings that she found both primitive and crude. Even more disconcerting to European taste was the presence of a huge bed standing foursquare in one corner of the room,

> with no lack of gold ornaments and of silk trappings ... that particular piece of furniture in a reception room always disturbs the idea of fitness in the eyes of a European.

She had very little leisure for further observation, as it was made plain that the queen was now graciously prepared to listen to her new musician. The piano had been placed just on the threshold of the main door, from which the ever-watchful monarch, who had not moved from her throne or balcony, could look down on both keyboard and player. Ida was indignant:

> This overbearing puffed-up woman seems really to believe herself a sacred being, raised above all the rest of the human race, and appears to think that it would derogate from her dignity to permit a stranger to come close to her.

Quietly fuming, and still under the queen's silent scrutiny, Ida walked forward alone, seating herself before the piano and striking a few preliminary chords – only to discover that the instrument was wildly and terrifyingly out of tune, with many keys failing even to produce a note when struck. Horribly aware of Ranavalona's notorious impatience and unmanageable tantrums, she was forced to spend long minutes hammering, loosening and lifting the recalcitrant keys, resorting to:

> all sorts of expedients to bring them into working order. And upon such an instrument as this I was to give my grand concert! But true artistic greatness rises superior to all adverse circumstances:

*and inspired by the thought of exhibiting my talents to such an appreciating audience, I perpetrated the most wonderful runs over the whole keyboard, thumped with all my might on the stubborn keys, and without any attempt at selection or sequence, played the first part of a waltz and the second of a march, in short anything and everything that came into my head.*

Sweating desperately, Ida finished her recital with a flourish and sat in trepidation, awaiting a response. But none came: no word of approbation, no polite applause greeted the final chord of the concert. There was a total absence of sound from the balcony. In the deafening silence, Ida rose from the piano and left, walking across the hushed courtyard back to her lodgings. It was not until much later that Prince Rakoto assured her that the queen had enjoyed every moment of the recital, especially the waltzes, and within a very short space of time would graciously allow her visitor to play before her again, though this time within the interior of the palace. By now, Ida seems to have begun almost to regret her involvement in the proposed coup, commenting wistfully (if perhaps a little drily) in her journal:

*Who knows, if the unhappy conspiracy had not occurred, if I might not have enjoyed the distinction of becomining* pianiste *to Her Majesty the Queen of Madagascar!*

That this farce was being played out between the two sides while at the same time they were engaged in a life or death struggle for supremacy merely serves to reinforce the surreal nature of life at the Merina court. Given the queen's network of spies and the eventual denouement of the coup, it is hard to avoid the conclusion that Ranavalona was privy to every part of the conspirators' plot. Secure in her ability to forestall the conspiracy, she may have taken pleasure in toying with the traitors as a cat plays with a mouse, giving balls in their honour, requesting concerts, knowing that at a time of her own choosing she would crush them beneath her claws. Ida suspected as much:

> Several times the thought has arisen in my mind, chiefly from the demeanour of Prince Raharo, that the Prince is surrounded by traitors, who pretend to acquiesce in his projects, but only do so to obtain a knowledge of them, and afterwards carry intelligence to the Queen.

Worse yet was the idea that the whole conspiracy had been allowed by the queen simply as a diversion for her wayward son, and that Ida's life now hung in the balance for nothing more than a royal pastime:

> Perhaps in this view they treat him like a child, and let him have his hobby, always, however, taking the necessary precautions to be able to stop his highness's sport before things go too far.

It was a ghastly concept, but the die was cast. There was simply no way to leave Madagascar at such short notice, the queen herself granting or denying such permission. And there was little point in leaving the capital for the countryside, even if permission to do so could be obtained. Having spent so much time in the conspirators' company, should the plot fail, Ida knew she would be singled out for Ranavalona's retribution no matter where she was on the island. Short of divulging the plot to the queen, she could see no possibility of turning back, and she suddenly found that she had very little time to reconsider her position. Three days after the piano recital, Lambert's fever abated and the plotters were ready to strike.

# CHAPTER TWENTY

# The Coup

**T**he conspirators had chosen the night of June 20 for the attempt and now Ida finally discovered the exact mechanism of the planned coup:

*The Prince was to dine at eight o'clock in the evening with M Lambert, Marius, Laborde and his son, in the garden-house belonging to the latter, and thither all reports from the other conspirators were to be carried, that it might be known if everything was progressing favourably, and that every man was at his post. At the conclusion of dinner, at eleven o'clock at night, the gentlemen were to march home to the upper part of the town, accompanied by music, as if they came from a feast; and each man was to remain quiet in his own house until two o'clock. At the latter hour all the conspirators were to slip silently into the palace, the gates of which Prince Raharo, the chief of the army, was to keep open and guarded by officers devoted to Prince Rakato; they were to assemble in the great courtyard, in front of the apartments inhabited by the Queen, and at a given signal loudly to proclaim Prince Rakato King. The new ministers, who had already been nominated by the Prince, were to explain to the Queen that this was the will of the nobles, the military, and the people; and at the same time the thunder of cannon from the Royal Palace was to announce to the people the change in the Government, and the deliverance from the sanguinary rule of Queen Ranavalona.*

It was clear that the whole scheme hinged on Prince Raharo's ability to control entrance to the palace to allow the conspirators to gather in the seat of government, to effectively take the queen into custody, and to make their proclamations. What Ida did not know was that a similar plot against the throne had been hatched in 1856, led by Prince Rakoto. This plan had also required that Prince Raharo secure the palace gates, but at the last moment the commander-in-chief had decided that his interests lay with the incumbent monarch and had refused to help. Some rumours claimed that this nobleman was a partisan of Prince Rakoto's rival for the succession, the formidable Prince Rambosalama, which might well explain his sudden volte-face. For Prince Rakoto, Laborde, Lambert and the rest of the conspirators to have depended on this broken reed for the success of their coup seems foolhardy in the extreme. They were risking everything – their wealth, their lives and the certainty of hideous torture – on the actions of this one man. It may be that the plotters had no option, however. As commander-in-chief, only Prince Raharo could guarantee them the entrance to the Palace on which the success of their plan depended. They simply had to trust him.

The order to begin the coup was sent out by runners to the lower-ranking members of the conspiracy. The plot's principals remained at their festive board, the lighted candles casting flickering shadows on their drawn, anxious faces. Fingers drummed nervously on table and armchair. Some paced restlessly up and down the room as the final minutes ticked slowly away; others sat immobile, staring sightlessly into the darkness, awaiting word of success or failure. But almost immediately, matters went awry.

In a nightmarish rerun of the previous plot, word reached the conspirators that 'in consequence of unforeseen obstacles' Prince Raharo had found it impossible to place officers devoted to Prince Rakoto in all areas of the palace. He was therefore unable to hold the palace gates open for the conspirators, and suggested that the coup should be deferred until a later date. At this there was uproar – they had already delayed too long; any further temporising would undoubtedly prove fatal. A note was hurriedly scribbled and sent off to the commander-in-chief, imploring him to continue with the plan, but with no response. A second letter was sent, with similar results.

*In vain did the Prince send messenger after messenger to him. He could not be induced to risk anything.*

Without control of the palace gates, nothing could be achieved. The revolution was cancelled.

With hindsight, the whole cabal was probably doomed from the outset. The large number of participants, the delays, the appalling lack of security and the conspirators' reliance on a man of proven timidity – each and every aspect of the plan argued for failure. It seems inconceivable that Ranavalona had no prior knowledge of the coup, and she may well have quietly orchestrated what was in fact a set-up, feigning ignorance of the intrigue in order to draw all the plotters out into the open. If so, the suppression of the coup had been most expertly handled: an overt revolution, even if crushed successfully, would clearly have produced a negative impact on the dignity of the crown, revealing to the populace the deep division between the queen and her son and heir, and between the monarchy and a large section of the aristocracy. Far better from Ranavalona's point of view to permit treason to prosper until all those who wavered from their loyalty could be identified, and then quietly and efficiently to quash the conspiracy before its revolutionary tendencies became manifest to the people. Stifled at birth, few would even know a coup had been planned, much less who the traitors were. But this was immaterial. Ranavalona would know. On the surface all would appear normal, while beneath the Great Queen could take her time in planning the final retribution, and perhaps find sport in playing mind games with her erstwhile conquerors.

This certainly seems to have been Ranavalona's preferred strategy. The day after the failed coup, Prince Rakoto brought word from his mother enquiring after her guests' well-being, and informing them that, as soon as M Lambert's health allowed it, she would wish to see he and Ida dancing together, perhaps demonstrating a new European dance for her entertainment. Ida confided to her journal:

> *A strange idea this! First I had to give a concert, and now I am to turn ballet-dancer, and perhaps afterwards dancing-mistress ... And Mr Lambert! What a thing to expect from a man who is still young, that he should execute a pas de deux with a women nearly sixty years old!*

The pair pleaded illness to escape the command performance, and the matter seems to have been dropped. But the incident gives a flavour of the surreal existence that Ida and the Frenchmen were experiencing at that time. Nothing was said, no action was taken against the Europeans and the feared arrests never materialised; but from the night of the failed coup, everything changed. From being honoured guests, the Europeans experienced a gradual, almost imperceptible slide towards the status of captives; and the worst of it was that there was absolutely nothing they could do. They were not even allowed to leave their dwelling, much less the capital, without the queen's express permission. Flight was impossible: the chance of a successful escape from the central highlands, through lands alive with the queen's supporters, was almost non-existent. It was made even less tempting by the fact that no overt hostility had so far been evinced against the conspirators. That the queen was angry there was no doubt, but there was always the possibility that, by not drawing attention to themselves, by maintaining a low profile within the capital, her anger would slowly burn itself out and she might turn her mind to other matters. Then again, she was just as likely to fall on them at any moment. The days dragged by in an agony of suspense:

> *July 2: What will become of us! The carrying out of the design seems to have become impracticable, for from the day when the Commander-in-Chief refused to open the doors of the palace, one after another the conspirators have fallen away, and traitors and spies surround us on all sides. Ever since the 20<sup>th</sup> June, hardly anyone associates with us; we are looked upon partly as state prisoners, and we are compelled to remain the whole day long in our houses, and dare not so much as set foot across the threshold.*
>
> *The best proof that the Queen is perfectly well-informed of the conspiracy, and only pretends to know nothing about it, for the sake of her son, of whom she is very fond, appears in the fact of her having, a few days since, forbidden every one, on pain of death, to make any accusation whatever against the Prince, or to impart any surmise of his guilt to her. This trait is worthy of the cunning character ... Having taken all necessary measures, and convinced herself that the power of the conspirators is broken, and that she has nothing to fear, she seeks to hide her son's fault from the people.*

Prince Rakoto brought word that the queen was consulting the oracles concerning their fate. While Lambert lay half-conscious, prostrated by a further attack of fever, she had visited the *sikidy* to discover if he truly harboured evil intentions against her reign. The soothsayer had performed the ritual and declared that Her Majesty need have no fear, for the gods would protect her: if Lambert plotted treason, then the fever would undoubtedly act in the queen's best interest and finish him off. She had accepted this prognostication, and Lambert had fortunately recovered his health. So now, their informants told them, the queen did not believe that they were involved in any plot against her. But in her anxious, paranoid state, Ida could not be comforted:

*Is this the truth? Or does the cunning woman only say it in the hope of worming something out of the Prince himself? Even if it is the truth, can she not consult the Sikidy over and over again, until, some fine day, it may give a different answer?*

Her worries were well founded. Early the next morning she heard that all the people had been summoned to appear at a grand *kabary* in the capital's central bazaar. In the past the convening of such assemblies had been prelude to terror and mass execution, and the news was greeted with dismay by the whole population.

*There was general howling and wailing, a rushing and running through the streets, as if the town had been attacked by a hostile army.*

Someone, though none was sure who, was about to pay for the abortive attempt on the throne.

It was death to ignore such a summons and the central forum of the capital was crowded with humanity when the hour of the *kabary* approached. Adding to the tension, the whole square had been surrounded by silent, grim-faced squadrons of heavily armed Merina troops. At the appointed time the queen's messenger arose, and in a loud and forceful voice delivered the word of his mistress, Ranavalona-Manjaka. The queen, he said, had long suspected that many members of that foreign religion, the Christians, had sprung up among her people, and within the past few days she had become aware that there were thousands of such converts in and around her capital. Everyone knew the contempt in which she held this sect, and how she had proscribed its rituals. They should know

> *that she would do her utmost to discover the guilty, and would*
> *punish them with the greatest severity; and that all should die*
> *who did not, within fifteen days, submit themselves to her*
> *pleasure.*

There were few takers of this offer. Just a few years before, a similar proclamation had been given, where the queen had threatened all Christians who attempted to hide their faith with death, but had promised that any who came forward to confess their 'crime' would not suffer the ultimate penalty. Several hundred took up her promise of an amnesty and voluntarily admitted their involvement in the foreign religion, hoping thereby to escape with their lives. And Ranavalona had kept her word – after a fashion. All those discovered to be Christians were indeed condemned to hideous deaths, by burning, boiling, flaying or being thrown from the rock at Ambohipotsy. As promised, those confessing were not actively slain. But Ranavalona had held to the letter rather than the spirit of her vow: she had them fastened together in groups of four, fettered about their necks with huge iron bars. Thus burdened, they had been set free to wander the countryside – accompanied by guards whose sole task was to prevent friends or relatives providing them with food or succour – until one by one they succumbed to fatigue and starvation. As the weakest died, the survivors of the quartet were obliged to drag the corpse along with them, hanging grotesquely by its neck between the emaciated bodies of the living. Few of those 'spared' by the queen survived the week.

The people knew that they could expect equal benevolence from their monarch on this occasion. Those who had seen her described her anger as terrible to behold: 'the Queen had never given way to such ungovernable outbursts of rage as now'. Her rage was compounded by the outpourings of the *sikidy*, whose priests she was consulting on an almost daily basis. The portents did not call for mercy: the spirits informed her that the coup was the work of the Christians on the island, and that nothing save the total extermination of the foreign religion could save the nation from chaos and her throne from destruction. It was a battle for survival that Ranavalona was determined to win; she became obsessed with a single resolute purpose, to obliterate once and for all the hateful sect from her realm.

A week after the *kabary*, Ida and Lambert believed that they were to be the first victims of the suppression. They had been warned that day, by a messenger from Prince Rakoto, to destroy all correspondence at once, for the queen's men were making their way to search the house for incriminating evidence, which would have led inevitably to their arrest on charges of treason. No sooner had this been done than the gates were flung open and around a dozen Merina officers, together with several troops of men, came into the courtyard:

> *We thought they were coming to make the search of which the Prince had warned us; but to our great astonishment, they explained to M Lambert that they had been sent by the Queen to receive the costly presents he had brought with him for her and her Court.*

Hiding his confusion and relief, Lambert immediately obliged, bringing out the chests containing the gifts, which were packed into great baskets and carried off by slaves who had accompanied the officers.

> *A few of the officers went away with the bearers; the others walked into our reception-room, conversed for a few moments with M Laborde and M Lambert, and then very politely took their leave.*

The Europeans were left stunned: there had been no search, no arrests. The officers had been polite and respectful. Was this a sign that the storm had abated? Had the queen relented?

Unfortunately, this episode proved merely to be a stay of execution, another example of Ranavalona's irrational (and perhaps intentional) schizoid behaviour, possibly designed to maintain the prisoners' state of mental disequilibrium. The queen's mercurial temperament shifted swiftly from thoughts of gifts to butchery, and a new round of killings began the next day, July 11, even before the end of the fifteen-day deadline she herself had set. That morning, Ranavalona's men dragged the first Christian victim, a frail old lady in her sixties, into the marketplace at Antananarivo, and gave her a most dreadful death – she was sawn to death.

This attack on the native Christians did not mean that the queen had forgotten the foreigners, the prime movers in the attempt to remove her from power. Even as her Christian subjects were being hauled away to deaths of awful and hideous variety, Ranavalona was contemplating the punishment of the outlanders. Six days after politely requesting her gifts from Lambert, on July 16, she secretly convened a *kabary* to determine his fate and that of the other Europeans. The *kabary* lasted an almost unprecedented six hours and by all accounts it was a turbulent and hard-fought debate. The argument was not over their guilt or innocence, for all present were convinced of the Europeans' culpability, but concerned their punishment. Nor was the basic sentence in doubt, for it was agreed unanimously that nothing short of death would suffice to exculpate their guilt. The debate appears to have centred around the important question of how the foreigners should die:

> *Some voted for a public execution in the market place, others for a nocturnal attack on M Laborde's house, while a third party proposed a banquet at which the Europeans were to be poisoned or murdered at a given signal.*

At the end of six hours, as the queen was on the point of deciding the manner of the Europeans' death, Prince Rakoto finally raised his voice. In the silence that ensued, he pleaded eloquently for the lives of his friends. He did not beg for mercy, but instead warned the queen that her rage and indignation were on the point of leading her to destruction. He pointed out that her government had only recently restored friendly trading relations with the western powers, and that economic sanctions would be the least result of the execution of the foreigners, expressing his conviction that Britain and France would use such an action as the perfect pretext to launch an attack on the country. The prince is said to have spoken with unheard-of energy, and indeed, being so intimately involved with the coup, he was taking an enormous risk in defending his friends. The queen heard his comments in stony silence.

For the Europeans, the waiting was proving intolerable. For almost two weeks they had been held in enforced passivity, utterly at the mercy of a brutal and ruthless autocrat, and their minds had become prey to myriad fears. Ida wrote in her journal:

> *For thirteen long days we have lived in the most trying suspense as to our impending fate, expecting every moment to hear some fatal news, and alarmed day and night at every slight noise. It was a terrible time.*

Above all, they craved certainty – a decision, any decision, was preferable to the limbo of doubt and terror that dominated their existence.

The morning of July 17 finally brought release from this awful suspense. While completing her notes Ida heard an unusual stir in the courtyard. She had no view of the area from her room and, full of trepidation, she hastily left her quarters, only to find Jean Laborde coming along the corridor to meet her. Quietly, he told her that a great *kabary* was being assembled in the courtyard of the house, which assembly all the Europeans had been commanded to attend.

> *We went accordingly, and found more than a hundred persons – judges, nobles and officers – sitting in a large half circle on benches and chairs, and some on the ground; behind them stood*

*a number of soldiers. One of the officers received us, and made us*
*sit down opposite the judges. These judges were shrouded in long*
*simbus, their glances rested gloomily and gravely upon us, and*
*for a considerable time there was deep silence. I confess to*
*having felt somewhat alarmed, and whispered to Monsieur*
*Laborde 'I think our last hour has come!'. His reply was, 'I am*
*prepared for everything'.*

The brooding atmosphere was finally broken when one of the
Judges arose and 'in sepulchral tones, embellished with a
multitude of high sounding epithets' revealed the fate of the
Europeans. The people had discovered, he said, that the foreigners
were republicans, and that they had come to Madagascar with
the express purpose of introducing a similar form of government
to the island. Their design entailed giving the commoners equal
rights to the nobles, abolishing slavery and, most heinous of
all, overthrowing their beloved ruler Ranavalona-Manjaka. In
addition, the Europeans had conspired with local Christians, 'a
sect equally obnoxious to the Queen and the people', bidding
them hold to their foreign beliefs and promising strong help
against their oppressors from abroad. Such traitorous dealings,
continued the judge in sombre tones, had so angered the
population and so turned them against the foreigners, that the
queen had been forced to place them in 'protective custody' in
order to secure their safety from the mob – the entire population
of the capital had demanded their execution.

Here the judge paused, and for a long moment a stillness like
death hung over the sunlit, dusty courtyard. Was it to be amnesty
or imprisonment, freedom or torture and annihilation? The
judge had begun speaking again. The queen was troubled and
angry, but

*as she had never yet deprived a white person of life, she would*
*abstain in this instance also, though the crimes ... committed*
*fully justified her in such a course. In her magnanimity and*
*mercy, she had accordingly decided to limit punishment to*
*perpetual banishment from her territories.*

It was an unlooked-for, and uncharacteristic, act of mercy from the Female Caligula. Only a short time was given to them for their departure. Ida, Lambert, M Marius and the two priests living at the house of Jean Laborde were allowed just one hour to leave the capital. In recognition of his past services to the state, Laborde was granted a full twenty-four hours to quit Antananarivo. In addition, he was allowed to take all his moveable possessions, with the exception of his slaves. These poor unfortunates, together with all Laborde's estates and houses, were forthwith confiscated by the crown. The queen had also taken thought for Laborde's son, and had decided that, as he was Malagasy on his mother's side and was too young to have taken a major part in the conspiracy, he might remain on the island should he choose or leave with his father.

Ranavalona gave orders to provide as many porters as required to allow the foreigners to carry away their property. And, using the excuse that they might require protection from the 'angry' populace on their journey to the coast, she insisted that a squadron of troops, fifty privates, twenty officers and a commandant, should accompany the exiles. Laborde was granted a similar number for his own escort, with the proviso that his party should always keep at least one day's march behind the rest of the Europeans.

While they had all avoided death, the sentence of banishment can only have come as a crushing blow to at least one of the Europeans. Jean Laborde had spent over twenty-six years on the island, had risen from slave to lover and confidant of the queen; he had been appointed a trusted counsellor to the court, and had almost single-handedly developed Madagascar's industrial base, in the process of which he had become an exceedingly wealthy man. And now, at a stroke, his fortune was gone and his life's work destroyed. But there was no help for it – it was bundle and go now, and given the queen's erratic and vindicative temperament, the sooner they were on the road to the coast the better. In just eight days they could be at Tamatave, where they might take ship for Mauritius and safety. There was always the chance that Ranavalona would change her mind and seek their deaths.

Ranavalona would not change her mind, though what was truly in her thoughts none of the Europeans came close to guessing. She was still mistress of Madagascar; the French plans to turn her beloved realm into a French protectorate had been thwarted and the instigators sent into exile. But it was not enough. The habits of more than three decades of sanguinary rule could not be denied – the queen still desired to revenge herself on the conspirators in the time-honoured way of her people. She wanted blood. Prince Rakoto's speech in defence of his friends had struck home, however. The foreigners could not simply be executed out of hand. Ranavalona was too astute a politician to ignore the perils of European intervention should anything untoward occur while they resided in her capital and she knew that she must stay her hand. But Madagascar's fever-ridden environment was acknowledged as a dangerous place for Europeans to live, and it was here that the queen saw a clandestine opportunity to obtain satisfaction. Ranavalona's insistence on an accompanying escort of Hova troops was no whim, but part of a carefully conceived plan to do away with her foreign enemies without incurring the wrath of their governments.

Despite the one-hour deadline, the foreigners were allowed to stay overnight in their homes. They left the following morning, but they did not reach the coast quite as early as anticipated. Instead of a rapid march to the coast, the queen's escort of soldiers forced delay after delay on the exiles. The Malagasy troops assigned to the party deliberately impeded progress as they crossed the most unhealthy portions of the route, so that the Europeans were constrained to spend long periods in the swamps and morasses of the malarial districts, and were lodged in the most horrendous conditions:

*Our progress from the capital to Tamatave was the most disagreeable and toilsome journey I have ever made; never, in all my various wanderings, had I endured anything like such suffering ... In the most pestiferous regions we were left in wretched huts for one or two weeks at a time; and frequently, when we suffered from violent attacks of fever, our escorts dragged us from our miserable couches, and we had to continue our journey whether the day was fine or rainy.*

At Beforona, a spot notorious for its fevers, the party was ordered to halt for a full 18 days. When they were finally allowed to move on, the party were fortunate to meet with a French physician from Reunion at the village of Eranomaro. But the Merina escort refused to countenance any contact, and the doctor was given no opportunity to alleviate the travellers' suffering. The soldiers were impervious to bribes, a strong indication of the emphasis the queen had placed on ensuring the demise of the *vazah* on their journey to the coast.

Ranavalona's reprieve, the mercy they had been granted at Antananarivo, was in reality a death sentence. Her plan was clearly to kill off the conspirators without actually executing them, in the hope of allaying the retribution of the European powers – if they died 'naturally' of disease how could she be held accountable? That this was a calculated attempt to kill off the foreigners cannot be doubted. The normal, week-long journey from Antananarivo to Tamatave was extended by these means to a murderous fifty-three days.

The stratagem worked. When the travellers at last reached the coast they were in a parlous state, all of them wasted by disease and scarcely able to walk. Ida Pfeiffer's sufferings were pitiable to see: the Madagascar fever was eating her up, draining her strength and energy hour by hour. She wrote in her journal:

*Every illness is trying, but the Madagascan fever is, perhaps, one of the most malignant of all diseases, and in my opinion it is far more formidable than the yellow fever or the cholera ... Violent pains are felt in the lower parts of the body, frequent vomitings ensue, with total loss of appetite and such weakness that the sufferer can hardly move a hand or foot. At last a feeling of entire apathy supervenes, from which the sick person is unable to rouse himself by even the strongest exertion of his will.*

The melancholy party finally embarked on Captain Schneider's brig *Castro* on September 16 and sailed for Mauritius, arriving at the island at 9 p.m. on September 22, after an arduous six-day voyage. Ida was taken to the house of a Mr Moon,

> *and to his, and to Dr Perrot's scientific skill and to the unceasing care bestowed upon me in his home, I have to ascribe my recovery; and it chanced that exactly on my sixtieth birthday, the 9<sup>th</sup> of October, 1857, I was pronounced out of danger.*

Even now, the indefatigable traveller refused to countenance a return home, and instead, after a few more months' convalescence, began planning a trip to Australia. But as she oversaw the loading of her gear onto her antipodean-bound vessel, the Madagascan fever returned with appalling suddenness to lay her low once more. Despairing of any further journeys, Ida finally agreed to a return to Europe and in March 1858 she quit Mauritius for London, from which she travelled to Hamburg and Berlin. Here she suffered a further collapse and she was carried back, in a special railway carriage and with the greatest care, to her home city of Vienna, arriving in a terribly weakened state in September.

It was obvious that something was very wrong. Her brother arranged several medical examinations by distinguished physicians and, as he reported in his additions to Ida's final book:

> *one and all pronounced that she was suffering from cancer in the liver – a consequence probably of the Madagascan fever; that the disease had deranged and was destroying the internal organs; and that her malady was incurable.*

The great traveller managed to cling on to life for a few more weeks, her pain lessened in the last few days by increasing doses of opiates, until 'in the night between the $27^{th}$ and $28^{th}$ of October, she expired peacefully, and apparently without pain'. Ranavalona's enmity had reached out across two continents to finally put paid to Ida's adventurous life.

Laborde and his compatriot Lambert both survived the gruelling trek from the capital. Lambert still held tightly to the charter granted him by Prince Rakoto, clinging to the slim hope that he might at some time return to Madagascar as a rich man, the owner of vast concessions. But for now they were banished men; while they had done their best to bring their schemes to fruition, all their plans had come to nought. They had set themselves against Ranavalona's cunning, and they had failed.

The Female Caligula had shown once again that she was capable of holding on to power in the Great Red Island. Not for the first time the French designs on the island had been held at bay. She had given

> a warning to Europeans that if the cautious policy of the Malagasy Government forbids the shedding of the white man's blood, yet there are other means of putting an end to foreign interference in the Government of the island.

And she had had her revenge.

CHAPTER TWENTY-ONE

# The Final Years

If the French adventurers (and the priests who accompanied them) had escaped with their lives, the same could not be said for the Christian converts they left behind. The persecution that had begun before the Europeans' banishment continued with even greater intensity after they had left the island. In the same month that Ranavalona pronounced the banishment of the *vazah* conspirators, towns and villages up and down the country were searched for prominent Christians, with death the reward for any Malagasy found harbouring the outcasts.

On one occasion a group of Christians were hidden in a pit covered by straw at a village house a few miles from the capital. Ranavalona's men had searched the house and were on the point of leaving, when the sound of a single muted cough produced renewed investigation, and the eventual capture of the fugitives. The officer in charge

> ordered the inhabitants of the village to be also bound and taken to
> the capital, for having afforded shelter and concealment to their
> friends ... The Queen was highly incensed against these villagers
> and commanded that every village should be searched, all the pits

*examined, and even the swamps and rivers dragged with nets,*
*rather than the Christians should remain in the land. So great*
*was the terror of the people, that the inhabitants of whole*
*villages fled.*

More than two hundred Christians were taken in this way, at
least half of whom suffered the extreme penalty. Fourteen of the
most prominent devotees of the foreign faith were executed at
Fiadana, about a mile distant from Ambohipotsy, by stoning to
death. This was a novel method of despatch at Imerina and it
was only poorly carried out: some of the condemned were still
breathing when their heads were cut from their bruised and
battered bodies and fixed to poles. Sixty or more were fettered
together in groups of up to seven individuals and left to die a
lingering, agonising death in their chains. A further fifty were
given the *tanguena* ordeal, from which eight were condemned
to death. All of those who survived were reduced to perpetual
slavery.

There is no doubt that the death toll would have been
much higher had it not been for the untiring efforts of Prince
Rakoto. Many of the Christians had been denounced by a single
informant, one Ratsimandisa, who had pretended to take on the
foreign faith and had abused his position of trust to compile a
comprehensive catalogue of all Christians living in the capital.
Hoping to curry favour with Ranavalona, he had handed this
list to a government minister to carry to the queen. By great
good fortune this man was a personal friend of the prince, and
presented it first to the crown prince for his perusal. Showing
great courage, Prince Rakoto immediately tore the paper to pieces,
and declared that any one

> *who dared to make out a second list of Christians, or even to*
> *accept one, with the intention of laying it before the Government,*
> *should be immediately put to death.*

He then sent word of the danger to all those under threat via his
friends and companions the *menamaso*. This prompt action slowed

the momentum of the persecutions and gave many families time to flee the capital and seek safety in the forests. Without his help, it is probable that hundreds more would have perished.

But the prince's aid for Christian converts did nothing to endear him to many of his fellow countrymen, who saw his humanitarian acts simply as another example of his subservience to the *vazah* and to their long-term plans for the subjugation of all Madagascar. Not a few considered the prince little short of a traitor to his people, which did not bode well for the queen's plans that her son should succeed her on the throne of Imerina.

Ranavalona had now ruled the Merina for thirty-three years; she already in her seventies and it was becoming obvious even to her most ardent supporters that the Great Glory was rapidly weakening. Not that there was the slightest admission by the queen that anything was amiss. Although she apparently favoured Prince Rakoto's succession as ruler of Imerina, she does not seem to have been able to acknowledge, even to herself, that her own reign, and with it her hold on absolute power, might be drawing to a close. Certainly, she made no attempt to remove herself gracefully from power by abdicating in favour of her son. Nor was there any let-up in the arbitrary arrests, the mutilations, the *tanguena* atrocities – if anything, the numbers despatched on the queen's orders increased during her declining years. But it was obvious to all that she could not be expected to maintain her iron grip on the country for much longer. And her demise would initiate the inevitable and long-delayed clash between the two princes, Rakoto and Rambosalama. At stake was the future of the Merina kingdom: would the country turn towards the modern world and engagement with the European powers with Rakoto as monarch, or remain in self-imposed traditional isolation under Rambosalama?

Both the rivals were backed by formidable groups of supporters. Rambosalama's campaign was underwritten by several ministers of state and by the chief judge of the nation; in addition, the pretender had continued the policy of using his substantial wealth to accumulate adherents or to bribe his way to influence, and many of the more mercenary nobles had rallied to his cause. By contrast, Prince Rakoto's interests were underpinned by several leading families, including the brothers Rainivoninahitraniony and Rainilaiarivony, the latter enjoying the position of commander-in-chief and able to bring the majority of the army to the aid of Ranavalona's only son. On balance, Prince Rakoto appeared to hold the advantage, but the political situation was delicately counterpoised and one careless move, or one act of boldness, might well tip the scales of success towards one or other of the rivals.

In the event it was the enterprising Rainivoninahitraniony, the true power behind Rakoto's faction, who struck first. The queen sickened visibly in August, and by the fifteenth of that month Ranavalona was confined to her bed, unable to command even herself and hourly expected to die. Rainivoninahitraniony was in constant contact with Prince Rakoto during this critical period and advised him by messenger to remain at the Tranovola, the Silver Palace, which adjoined the main palace, the Manjakamiadana, built by the now exiled Jean Laborde. Rainivoninahitraniony ordered three hundred of his most loyal troops to surround the Silver Palace and stationed further squads all around the Manjakamiadana, which effectively denied Rambosalama's supporters entrance to the royal grounds from which, by tradition, decrees concerning the kingship were proclaimed. Even as these steps were being taken, other messengers had been despatched to Prince Rakoto's supporters throughout Imerina, commanding their presence, under arms, in the capital the following day.

Then, as darkness descended and while the queen still breathed, the astute prime minister persuaded Prince Rakoto to appear on the balcony of the palace dressed in royal robes to acknowledge the loyal salutations of the assembled soldiers in the courtyard. As the prince–king retired for the night additional troops were dispatched, under cover of darkness, to secure the Tampombohitra, the strategically important topmost area of the capital. Nothing was left to chance. Through Rainivoninahitraniony's nephew, Radriaka, who was an officer of the palace, it was arranged for news of the queen's death to be communicated the moment it occurred. With all these precautions in place, Rainivoninahitraniony retired to his bed.

Tradition states that the night brought strange signs and omens of the queen's imminent demise. Strange lights were seen in the hills, moving slowly, like a torchlit procession marching at foot pace across the mountains. But when soldiers were sent to investigate the area, they found nothing. For the superstitious, this was an infallible harbinger of the end: Ranavalona's soul, they said, had already left her body and was being carried in procession towards the twelve hills of her ancestors. Later that same night, sad and soulful music was heard emanating from the mausoleum of Renihar on the lower slopes of the town. Slowly, over the space of an hour, the doleful sounds mounted upwards through the streets of the capital, moving towards the Rova, the royal palace on the topmost crag of Antananarivo. And it was said that, at the very moment the spectral tones reached the palace gates, the queen's soul left her body.

It was 7.30 a.m., August 15, 1861. Ironically enough for such a brutal and violent monarch, Ranavalona died peacefully in her sleep. She had reigned over Madagascar for thirty-three years, had been responsible for the death of at least a third of the island's population, and by the time she expired was probably insane. But, unlike many other African and Asian kingdoms, while Ranavalona held power Madagascar had successfully defied all attempts at colonisation. The island had remained an independent state despite the best efforts of both Britain and, especially, France to bring it under European sway. For all her manifold faults, the Female Caligula had fulfilled the sacred promises she had made more than three decades before, standing proudly on the sacred coronation stone as the young and beautiful Queen of Imerina:

> Never say 'she is only a feeble and ignorant woman, how can she rule such a vast empire'. I will rule here, to the good fortune of my people and the glory of my name! I will worship no gods but those of my ancestors. The Ocean shall be the boundary of my realm and I will not cede the thickness of one hair of my realm!

# Epilogue

**P**rime Minister Rainivoninahitraniony's response to the queen's death was immediate. He rushed to the palace, where his brother Rainilaiavirony had already taken Prince Rakoto, and there, on Ranavalona's balcony, the prince was proclaimed ruler of the Imerina under the title of King Radama II. Soldiers were immediately despatched to escort Rambosalama to the palace, where his allegiance was demanded, with the unspoken threat that his death was inevitable should he refuse. The pretender must have seen that his position was untenable, for he submitted to the oath of allegiance without protest. With all opposition effectively quashed and the palace grounds secure, Raharolahy was sent to the main market of the capital and to the *kabary* ground of Andohalo, where the new king's accession was proclaimed to the populace.

Several groups of Prince Rambosalama's supporters had been discovered under arms when Rakoto's own adherents attempted a round-up of likely opposition groups. Using this resistance as a pretext, a number of the king's advisers

*counselled the death of Rambosalama as essential to the peace of the country and the king's own safety. But Radama II would not*

*consent, and only agreed to banish his rival to Ambohimirimo,*
*one of his own villages, sixteen or twenty miles west of the capital.*

The new king may have learnt from his mother in this, and his
apparent restraint may well have been more an example of
delayed retribution. Within a short while the young, vigorous
pretender to the throne of Imerina had become ill. Eight months
after the date of Prince Rakoto's accession he was dead. The cause
was never specified, but many suspected poison.

The new king's coronation was a sumptuous affair, attended
by all the Merina nobility, tribal representatives from across
the island and several high-ranking foreign missions, including
Britain and France. The king wore a field marshal's uniform of
British design, and as if to symbolise the balance he wished to
show towards the two main colonial powers, his queen was
dressed in an elaborate Parisian gown, the personal gift of the
French Emperor. The ceremony was celebrated with much pomp
on the plains of Mahamasina, close to Ambohipotsy, where so
many Christian martyrs had perished under the reign of Rakoto's
mother. The fetish priests seized the opportunity to parade the
*sampy,* the thirteen ancestral gods of Imerina, before the people,

> *carried on tall slender rods or poles, from eight to ten feet*
> *high ... Dirty pieces of silver chain, silver balls varying in size*
> *from a pistol bullet to a hen's egg, pieces of coral and what*
> *seemed like bone and silver ornaments intended to represent*
> *crocodile's teeth, and with these narrow strips of scarlet cloth,*
> *from a foot to a yard or more in length, some of them*
> *underneath what looked like a red woolen cap, resembling a cap*
> *of liberty; others invisible, consisting of something tied up in a*
> *small bag of native cloth or rush basket; such were the obects of*
> *worship, or the representatives of such, on which the safety and*
> *welfare of the nation were supposed to depend.*

But no longer. Crowned as King of Madagascar, with both his mother and his rival safely interred and with the country now securely under his control, Radama II did not long delay the implementation of his modernising agenda. Just as Ranavalona had effectively reversed the policies of her husband, the former monarch Radama I, so now did her son, Radama II, overturn almost all of her own long-cherished edicts.

Many of the worst excesses of Ranavalona's brutal rule were immediately eliminated. The *tanguena* and other trials by ordeal were abolished, and numerous aspects of the corrupt judicial sytem reformed. Lands confiscated by the queen for real or imagined misdemeanours were returned to their owners, a policy that aided many Christian converts of all ranks. In addition, the king greatly reduced the demands of the *fanompoana*, the hated corvée or forced labour used for royal or public works, and instead began the practice (unheard of in Imerina before that time) of paying the workmen for their labour. The Merina soldiery, who previously had to drill and train – at their own expense – every two weeks, were now required to report only every two months, a sure sign that the king planned no new conquests or raids against his neighbours.

In a further unprecedented move, the new king ordered the release of all captives taken from the Betsileo, Sakalava and other tribes during the numberless predatory expeditions sent forth in previous years by his ruthless mother. The bones of those who had died in captivity were also returned to their homeland to be buried according to traditional rites. This open-handed treatment of former enemies produced the most gratifying response from the neighbouring tribal people. Instead of rebelling from the yoke of the Merina, many tribes to the west and south voluntarily tendered their allegiance to the new monarch, and the remaining independent Sakalava tribe sent ambassadors to the Merina capital for what turned out to be amicable discussions and the pledging of nominal allegiance. In a reciprocal gesture, these talks led to Merina captives, taken by Sakalava warriors during Ranavalona's reign, being returned to their own land. As a result, the borderlands between Sakalava and Merina territory, scarred by years of conflict and devoid of villages and people, began to fill up with new settlers from both ethnic groups, and the land once again became fruitful.

In parallel with this enlightened 'foreign' policy, one of Radama II's first acts was to grant all citizens of his kingdom, and all foreign visitors, complete freedom of religion. Despite the universal tolerance of this proclamation, its main beneficiary was Christianity, at the expense of the traditional native beliefs. The diktat effectively removed all proscriptions from the practice of Christianity (which had been the main casualty of Ranavalona's persecutions). And by allowing the rearing of swine in the capital, whose presence was taboo to the 'idols', the king forced the exile of the traditional fetish priests and their gods to the countryside, where their chances of fomenting disorder were greatly reduced. Radama II also allowed the return of the missionaries with their schools and churches to all parts of the country, including the capital. The fetish priests and idol keepers were incensed, but could only nurse their hatred as the despised foreign religion once more began to claim converts by the thousand. The policy also had its downside, however, for on seeing the influence of the foreigners waxing strong, many citizens of Imerina began to fear for their traditional independence, and such anxieties could only play into the hands of the fetish priests and their supporters.

Further exacerbating these fears, along with the missionaries all foreign traders were also granted favoured status. Radama II wrote to the governors of both Reunion and Mauritius, inviting entrepreneurs and settlers to his realm, assuring them of a fine welcome. They would, he promised, be free to set up plantations and to trade freely. Just one exception was made: true to his non-violent principles, he banned only the trade in arms and ammunition. As an added incentive to commerce, the king abolished all import and export duties on all goods. The manner in which he did this gives some indication of the power the former Prince Rakoto now wielded, and how little some things had actually changed in Imerina. Absolutism still ruled supreme. The whole economy of the nation was changed overnight simply by the force of the king's word, epitomised by the terse two-line missive he sent to the governor of Mauritius:

*To His Excellency the Governor of Mauritius,*

*Antananarivo 20th August, 1861*

*Being Sovereign of Madagascar, I have ordered the governors at my different ports not to get any duties from the things imported and exported.*

*Radama II*
*King of Madagascar*

Much might have altered following the death of the queen, but it was obvious that the concept of divine rule remained alive and vigorous. Unfortunately, this autocratic decision to revoke all customs duties was not merely undemocratic, it proved to be disastrous, both for the reforms that Radama II hoped to institute and for his rule.

Many of the nobles on whom Radama II relied for support obtained much of their income from customs duties, licit or illicit, and they were not pleased to see their fortunes destroyed overnight. The reduction of the corvée system had already alienated a considerable proportion of the nobility, who looked on the practice as a long-standing privilege of their class, and they were loath to relinquish yet another of their traditional rights on the whim of a modernising monarch. Abolishing the customs duties was a dreadful error, and could only further undermine the king's power base. The decision also resulted in an absolute flood of 'spiritous liquors' into the country, brandy from Reunion and rum from Mauritius. Previously, the duty imposed had pushed the price high and kept these products out of reach of all but the most wealthy. Now rum became available to all and excess was the order of the day; the missionary William Ellis was appalled to find that one in every four houses in the villages he passed was a rum shop, with almost all the inhabitants in varying degrees of intoxication.

Seeing their people debauched and noting the loss of personal revenue, some members of the aristocracy began openly to question the direction in which their new king was steering the country. The foreigners were making greater and greater inroads into the commerce of the nation, they were in the counsels of the king, their missionaries had begun again to preach their foreign god. Was Radama II leading the nation to ruin?

As if in answer, just one year into the rule of their new monarch, a terrible judgement was visited on the nation. Plague struck the country, reaching out indiscriminately to carry off noble, slave and labourer in its cold embrace. The diseased ravaged the capital for weeks, devastating its population. For many it was the judgement of heaven: they attributed the malady to the anger of the gods and their ancestors at Radama II's love of foreign ways and his submissive attitude to the colonial powers. This alone would have undermined the king's position, but it was accompanied, at almost the same time, by an eruption of *imanenjana*, a species of chorea similar to the medieval St Vitus' dance, in which the victims were seized with an unstoppable urge to leap and spring about in jerky, spasmodic movements. The Malagasy regarded the phenomenon as possession by the ancestral spirirts, and many of the sufferers openly proclaimed that they were animated by the spirit of the Great Glory herself, that Ranavalona's ghost had descended on them from the land of the shades, to show her anger and opposition to the abandonment of traditional ways.

In the face of these two apparently supernatural omens, many felt their loyalty to the king waver, and some secretly transferred their allegiance to men they felt more capable of emulating the late queen and facing down the foreign aggressors.

Rainivoninahitraniony, the king's Machiavellian prime minister and the true eminence grise within the palace hierarchy, was among those who felt, and sympathised with, this shift in sentiment. Casting round for another worthy occupant for the throne of Imerina, he found few who might merit the honour. And in line with many other capable men throughout history, he began to wonder if he himself might not be the best man to return the Merina to their former greatness.

The worsening situation appears to have had a damaging effect on the king, for his personality seemed to undergo a noticeable alteration during this period, becoming markedly more intemperate. This was most clearly seen in his response to a violent argument that broke out between one of his companions, the *menamaso*, and Rainivoninahitraniony. The matter could not be amicably resolved, so Radama, having heard of the European fashion for the duel, proposed that the two should resort to arms to settle the issue. This suggestion went against all Malagasy traditions, but so taken was Radama by the idea, that he then declared that he would issue a decree to force all individuals, clans and even entire settlements to submit their differences to trial by combat.

How a king who had banned trading in arms and had recently proscribed the appalling *tanguena* ordeal could now unblushingly promote such a bloody and violent 'solution' to disagreements was as inexplicable then as it is today, and it made many doubt the king's sanity. The proposed decree united the whole government in opposition, and on the dark and misty morning of May 8, 1863, they made their way en masse towards the royal Rova to beg the king to reconsider. But Radama remained adamant. He was king, he ruled Madagascar by decree and by divine right, and ordeal by battle would become the law of the land.

This obdurate, unyielding attitude drove Radama's remaining loyal followers from their allegiance, including most of the military. They had already seen the *menamaso* and the foreigner elevated to positions of prestige and influence, while they had suffered loss of income, status and privilege. And now this. What new humiliations might face them if they refused to act?

The morning after their abortive meeting with the king, on the orders of Rainivoninahitraniony the chief minister, soldiers of the Merina army flooded in to the capital. Quickly they searched out the king's companions, the *menamaso*, and slaughtered them to a man. Several *menamaso* sought protection with the king in his quarters. Radama II bargained for their safety and, when promised that their lives would be spared if they surrendered, reluctantly handed his friends over to the rebellious troops. The men were immediately pinioned and speared to death. None of the missionaries or European traders was hurt. Knowing the consequences of offending the colonial powers, the foreigners were left untouched.

But having isolated the king by the murder of his friends, Rainivoninahitraniony and his allies found that they had brought on themselves an even greater problem. The group had acted in order to save their positions and rank, but how could they continue to serve a king they had in all but name rebelled against, whose friends they had murdered, and at whose word they could be sentenced to death without hope of reprieve? The answer was obvious. If they wished to survive, the king must die.

Three days after the murder of the *menamaso* a band of assassins broke into the royal quarters and, before the horrified eyes of Queen Rasoherina, Radama II was struck to the ground. The king was savagely kicked and beaten, but none of the assassins seems to have been prepared to break the ancient taboo against spilling the royal blood. Radama was finally given his quietus by strangulation with a silken cord. The regicides then threw the body onto a cart and ordered it carried to the village of Ilafy, some miles to the north-east of the capital, and buried in an unmarked grave.

At first, it was announced that the king had died by his own hand. But later, as rumours of the murder circulated and the fear of reprisal increased, the conspirators attempted to profit from the undoubted xenophobia of the nation at that time, and to use the stories of the king's mixed-blood ancestry as a pretext for his assassination. Truth or convenient fiction, it was given out that the king had been 'retired' because he was no true Merina, but a mulatto, the illegitimate son of the late queen and the exiled Frenchman Jean Laborde.

The king's assassination was by no means greeted with universal approval. Like with many another popular monarch, the common people of Imerina were incensed by his enforced 'retirement' and many refused to believe that he had died. The rumour arose that he had survived strangulation, that he had regained consciousness on the road to Ilafy, and that the escort charged with burying his body had allowed the newly resurrected monarch to make his escape into the forest. It was said that Radama was living in hiding in the remote north-west of the country, plotting his return when circumstances allowed. Several insurrections against the plotters followed, each of them, it was rumoured, led by the deposed king.

The story of the king's survival may well have had some truth in it – certainly both William Ellis and Jean Laborde believed that Radama had not perished on the night of his purported assassination – and a curious incident in May 1864 leant great credence to the myth that was developing around the missing king. Following a particularly widespread conspiracy, seventy-nine individuals were arrested and charged with claiming that the king was still alive. Even when faced with the death penalty, sixteen of the captives refused to recant, and all went to their deaths proclaiming that they had seen the king alive and well in the Malagasy forests.

After September 1864 there were no further sightings of the king. He may, as a later biographer claimed, have simply despaired of ever regaining his throne and retreated into a secure obscurity. It is doubtful if we will ever know the full story of the king's overthrow, but from this time on Ranavalona's only son disappeared forever from the stage of Madagascan history, and with him any real hope of modernising reforms.

With the death of the 'true king', the story of Madagascar's royal line becomes one of steady decline, of a country ruled by a series of *reines fainéants* (enfeebled queens), token figures of royalty whose powers and authority were exercised in secret by others.

Rainivoninahitraniony moved quickly to consolidate his position after the assassination. Within a few weeks he had married Queen Rasoherina, the late king's wife, a traditional method for usurpers to legitimise their rule. But it was all in vain, for once a crown is stolen, that intimidating, sacrosanct quality of kingship and lineage is also destroyed, and the royal dignity becomes less an object of numinous awe than a possession to be seized by any resolute or artful ruffian.

As the weeks went by it became obvious that Rainivon-inahitraniony had arrogated to himself the privileges of a divine ruler: he acted with arrogance and pride towards his former friends, and resorted to violence if his commands were questioned. Shortly after the plot of May 1864, he demanded the deaths of all seventy-nine captured rebels who continued to espouse Radama II's survival. When this was opposed by the queen, the majority of the government, and even his own brother Rainilaiarivony, he lashed out at the veteran minister Rainijohary, striking him, and menaced the others with a drawn sword. At around the same time he threatened his brother and a number of other nobles with a spear, though in mitigation he was probably drunk at the time, for along with his other faults Rainivoninahitraniony's addiction to the bottle was fast becoming legendary.

These outbursts turned even his own family against him, and they petitioned the queen to remove their recalcitrant relation, requesting that Rainivoninahitraniony's brother, Rainilaiarivony, be allowed to take his place. The queen had already been forced to drink alcohol by her unstable husband (in direct contravention of Malagasy law) and she quickly acceded to their appeal. A royal message was delivered to Rainivoninahitraniony informing him that as, because of ill health, he had made known his desire to step down from the cares of office, the queen had graciously decided to agree to his request.

Rainivoninahitraniony took his sudden deposition well, and made a dignified and immediate withdrawal to his country estate. But the incident shows how great the traditional power of the monarch remained; a power that, had Queen Rasoherina possessed her aunt Ranavalona's iron will and fiery temperament, might well have seen the return of a second Female Caligula and a renewed spirit of Malagasy independence. As it was, after this brief outburst of royal authority the queen returned to her normal supine ways, and allowed herself to be passed, like some docile possession, from one brother to another. Rainilaiarivony married her in 1869.

Three years later, Queen Rasoherina was dead. Yet another obscure niece of Ranavalona was now thrust forward and proclaimed queen, only to be immediately fettered in the bonds of matrimony by the artful Rainilaiarivony. She ruled, a simple mouthpiece for Rainilaiarivony's commands, under the title Ranavalona II. The irony may or may not have been intentional, but the contrast between this puppet monarch and the rule of Ranavalona can hardly have been more pronounced.

Constant intrigue and the lack of strong royal leadership meant that Rainilaiarivony increasingly ruled over a land divided among itself. And taking advantage of the internal feuding and incipient schism, the *bête noir* of Malagasy independence returned to haunt the usurpers. The shade of Ranavalona may perhaps have smiled wryly at the nemesis that now stalked the killers of her son – the French were again casting covetous eyes on the Great Red Island.

France had maintained its long-standing interest in Madagascar for more than two hundred years, and even during the recurring periods of British influence had never abandoned its colonial ambitions for the island. But the French had always been held in check by British foreign policy, which would not countenance a protectorate of its colonial rival that lay across the strategically important trade route between Britain's domains in South Africa and British India. All this was swept away in 1874 with the opening of the Suez Canal: India and the Far East could now be accessed faster and more securely from the Mediterranean, and at a stroke the passage around the Cape of Good Hope lost much of its significance. Quite suddenly, the French found they had a much freer hand with Madagascar.

In 1878 that adventurous Gascon, Jean Laborde, died in Madagascar, where he had held the post of French Consul since 1862. He left much land and property on the island, and the French immediately seized on a dispute that arose over this inheritance as a pretext for another attempt on Madagascan independence. The attack was spurred on by the 'Touale incident' of May 1881, when a French-owned gun-running dhow, discovered in Malagasy waters, was involved in a firefight with Merina troops and several of its Arab crew were killed. Although selling arms was in direct contravention of the Franco-Malagasy treaty signed that same year, and the crew of the dhow had themselves initiated hostilities, the French demanded compensation. A Malagasy embassy to France, Britain and the USA in 1882 failed to resolve the situation, and within twelve months French troops had attacked the island and occupied several ports. That same year Ranavalona II died of illness; needless to say Rainilaiarivony had a successor in the wings, another little-known relative of Ranavalona who received the title Ranavalona III, and whom he quickly married to maintain his position.

The Franco-Malagasy war continued for nearly two and a half years, but without the arsenal of Mantasoa to furnish home-produced arms and powder, it was from the start an unequal battle; it ended with the French dominant and able to dictate terms for a harsh treaty making Madagascar a form of French protectorate. Rainilaiarivony used all his wiles to avoid full acceptance of this status, dragging his diplomatic heels while hoping desperately for British support; but Her Britannic Majesty's government had lost interest in Madagasacar and in 1890 signed away its involvement in the Convention of Zanzibar.

The French now continued their advance across the island, and on September 30, 1895, a flying column of 4,000 French troops supported by twelve mountain howitzers made the final asssault on the capital Antananarivo. The royal Rova fell after a brief and bloody fight and, 253 years after the first Frenchman had landed at Fort Dauphin in 1642, the Great Red Island was finally in their hands.

For twelve months Madagascar remained a full protectorate, but in 1896 it became what the French had always intended it should be, a French colony. A year later the monarchy was abolished, and ex-Queen Ranavalona III was exiled to Algeria.

It was the end of all that the Female Caligua had held dear. During her long reign Ranavalona-Manjaka had successfully sustained the culture she had inherited: she had extended her domains and, against the colonial current of the times, had kept the island free from foreign influence. But on her demise all these achievements melted away in the furnace of factional intrigue and external aggression. Madagascar's independence as a sovereign state had perhaps demanded the rule of a Sanguinary Queen, but the bloodline of Andrianampoinimerina and Radama never again produced a monarch of Ranavalona's political skill and ruthlessness. The industrial factories of Mantasoa, the architectural glories of the Black Versailles, the pomp and spectacle of Merina royalty, all sank into oblivion after her death. French became the national language, and the compliant populace rapidly converted from animism and Protestantism to follow the Church of Rome. Ranavalona's legacy was finally, and completely, extinct.

# Selected Bibliography

The story of Madagascar has recently become a growing topic of research among historians and anthropologists. Unfortunately, most of the work is rather recondite and of narrow focus, and can be found only in obscure learned journals. Most is written in French. The selected bibliography below lists the most accessible and important books and articles.

Ayache Simon (ed.) 1981. *Histoire Fianarantsoa: Imp.Catholique.* (A secret history recorded by a secretery to Ranavalona I, and a high noble).

Ayache Simon (ed) 1965. *L'accession au trône, 1828, de ranavalo Iere a travers le témoignage de raombana, 1854.* 1965.

Berg, Gerald. 1985. The Sacred Musket. *Comparative Studies in Society and History* 27/2: 261–279. (An analysis of the role of guns in l8th century political change).

Brown, Mervyn. 1979. *Madagascar Rediscovered.* Hamden, CT: Archon. (An excellent modern-day history of the island).

Callet, François. 1912 *Histoire des Rois Antananarivo*: Academie Malgache. (French text of the royal traditions of Imerina.)

Deschamps, Hubert. 1965. *Histoire de Madagascar.* Paris: Berger-Levrault. (Probably the best general historical study.)

Ellis, William. 1838. *History of Madagascar*. Fisher. (Includes first-hand account of Ranavalona and her reign. Many believe Ellis recorded direct translations of Merina traditions with far less impact from European historiography than following works). London.

Ellis, William. 1867. Madagascar Revisited; describing the events of a new reign, and the revolution which followed; setting forth also the persecutions endured by the Christians. London.

Ellis, William. 1870. *The Martyr Church: a narrative of the introduction, progress and triumph of Christianity in Madagascar, with notices of personal intercourse and travel in that island*. London.

de Flacourt, Etienne. 1661 *Histoire de la Grande Île* (reprinted in Collections des Ouvrages concernant Madagascar, 9 : 1–246).

Harry, Miriam. 1939. *Ranavalo et son amant blanc*. Paris. (an excellent book for local colour, but rather given to romantic flights of fancy).

Heseltine, Nigel. 1971. *Madgascar*. London: Pall Mall. (Good recent overview of the Great Red Island).

Kottak Conrad 1971. Cultural Adaptation, Kinship, and Descent in Madagascar' *Southwest Journal of Anthropology*, 27: 129–147.

Macloed, L. 1865. *Madagascar and Its People*. London.

Oliver, S. P. 1886. *Madagascar, an historical and descriptive account of the island and its former dependencies*. MacMillan. London.

Pfeiffer Ida Laura. 1852. *A Lady's Travels Around the World*. (trans: W Hazlitt) G Routledge and Co. London.

Pfeiffer, I. L. 1855. *A Lady's Second Journeys Round the World*. (trans: J Sinnett). 2 Volumes. London.

Pfeiffer, O. (ed.). 1861. *The Last Travel of Ida Pfeiffer, inclusive of a visit to Madagascar*. (trans: H. W. Dulcken). Routledge, Warne and Routledge. London.

Sibree, James. 1880. The Great African Island. Trubner and Co. London. (excellent for geography of the island, but very little historical coverage).

# Index